Praise for The S

'A timely book for th   the
tough seasons of life
James Lawrence, CPAS le

'This is not a book to ̶   ̶ ̶ ̶ ̶ ̶ ̶ ̶ ̶ ̶ ̶ ̶ got Gems keep tumbling out of
the cupboard and they need to be picked up one at a time before
moving to the next... This is hard to beat!'
Julian Henderson, bishop of Blackburn

'A wonderfully honest and human book that enables readers to find
God in the disturbing experiences of change and disruption... The
rich wisdom of this book will offer both a healing balm and a source
of courage to all who engage with it.'
Philip North, bishop of Burnley

'This book is important... It tackles difficult times in our lives with
honesty and clarity – which will be a relief to those who read it.'
Canon Dr Christina Baxter

'This book draws on the Bible, on the lives of saints old and new,
and on the author's deep experience to invite us afresh to engage
in the precious things God is doing when the temptation is to focus
elsewhere. This is encouraging, wise, and helpful.'
Mark Tanner, bishop of Chester

'In a highly engaging way, Mark extends our awareness and draws
our attention to God's work of grace in the whole of life – not only
the highs and lows, but the rest of life, where we are on a journey,
waiting, confused or disoriented. This is a guide for a truly whole-life
discipleship.'
Paul Harcourt, New Wine national leader and vicar of All Saints Woodford Wells

'An apt resource and encouragement that we are not alone in
experiencing these seasons.'
Jo McKee, CPAS director of the Arrow Programme and archbishops' evangelist,
vicar of St Andrew's Radcliffe

The Bible Reading Fellowship
15 The Chambers, Vineyard
Abingdon OX14 3FE
brf.org.uk

The Bible Reading Fellowship (BRF) is a Registered Charity (233280)

ISBN 978 0 85746 825 3
First published 2021
10 9 8 7 6 5 4 3 2 1 0

Text © Mark Bradford 2021
This edition © The Bible Reading Fellowship 2021
Cover image © Joe Gardner on Unsplash
Inside illustrations © Karen Fowler

The author asserts the moral right to be identified as the author of this work

Acknowledgements
Unless otherwise acknowledged, scripture quotations are taken from The Holy
Bible, New International Version (Anglicised edition) copyright © 1979, 1984, 2011
by Biblica. Used by permission of Hodder & Stoughton Publishers, a Hachette
UK company. All rights reserved. 'NIV' is a registered trademark of Biblica. UK
trademark number 1448790. • Scripture quotations marked NRSV are taken from
The New Revised Standard Version of the Bible, Anglicised edition, copyright ©
1989, 1995 by the Division of Christian Education of the National Council of the
Churches of Christ in the United States of America. Used by permission. All rights
reserved.

p. 7: Judy Brown, 'Fire', reproduced with permission from Judy Brown, *A Leader's
Guide to Reflective Practice* (Trafford, 2006), p. 4. • p. 61: Marlo Schalesky, 'A prayer
for when you're stuck in the waiting place', reproduced with permission. • p. 139:
James Martin, 'A prayer in the storm', reprinted from America October 28, 2012
with permission of America Press, Inc., 2012. All rights reserved. • p. 163: Ann
Weems, 'Lament Psalm One', reproduced with permission from Ann Weems,
Psalms of Lament (Westminster John Knox Press, 1995), pp. 1–2.

Every effort has been made to trace and contact copyright owners for material
used in this resource. We apologise for any inadvertent omissions or errors, and
would ask those concerned to contact us so that full acknowledgement can be
made in the future.

A catalogue record for this book is available from the British Library

Printed and bound by CPI Group (UK) Ltd, Croydon CR0 4YY

Mark Bradford

THE
SPACE
BETWEEN

**The disruptive seasons
we want to hide from,
and why we need them**

To all who know the pain of the space between,
that it might become for them a place of hope and new life.

Contents

Acknowledgements 6

'Fire' by Judy Brown 7

1   Introduction 8

2   Two disruptive moments in the life of Jacob 23

3   The time of waiting: when life is put on hold 35

4   The place of exile: when life feels alien 62

5   The wilderness: when life is stripped back 90

6   The storm: when life is shaken 114

7   The pit: when life sinks to the bottom 140

8   Conclusion 166

Words from Karen Fowler, illustrator 184

Notes 185

Acknowledgements

Thanks to…

… Olivia, Rachel and all at BRF for their work on the book, especially during these difficult past twelve months.

… Anne King, Elise and Michael Hutchinson, Peter and Jackie Scott, Kevin and Karen Fowler, Jane Knoop and Bridget Bradford for their help in reading through the text and offering corrections to it.

… Marlo Schalesky and Judy Brown for the very kind use of their work.

… the friends who have shared so personally of themselves in the 'contemporary saints' sections. I'm deeply moved at the ways in which they model in practice the honesty and hope that this book points towards.

… Karen Fowler for her wonderful illustrations throughout the book and her words at the end.

… the churches of Holy Trinity Ripon, St Cuthbert's Church Fulwood in Preston and Pudsey Parish Church in Leeds, as well as the Preston Area Churches Lent Series, who have all listened to parts of this book in various talks, helping to shape its content. I'm so grateful to those at Holy Trinity and St Cuthbert's in particular for being places of such welcome to us as a family.

Last, but most important, I'd like to thank Sarah, Caleb, Anna and Phoebe for their endless love and support that keeps me going in everything, and without which this book, and so much else, would not be possible.

'Fire' by Judy Brown

What makes a fire burn
is space between the logs,
a breathing space.
Too much of a good thing,
too many logs
packed in too tight
can douse the flames
almost as surely
as a pail of water would.
So building fires
requires attention
to the spaces in between,
as much as to the wood.

When we are able to build
open spaces
in the same way
we have learned
to pile on the logs,
then we can come to see how
it is fuel, and absence of the fuel
together, that make fire possible.
We only need to lay a log
lightly from time to time.
A fire
grows
simply because the space is there,
with openings
in which the flame
that knows just how it wants to burn
can find its way.[1]

1

Introduction

**Jesus answered, 'I am the way and the truth and the life.
No one comes to the Father except through me.'**
JOHN 14:6

**Between stimulus and response, there is a space. In the space
there is the power to choose our response. In our response lies
our growth and our freedom.**
Author unknown[2]

Oh, the grand old Duke of York, he had ten thousand men.
He marched them up to the top of the hill and he marched them
down again.
And when they were up, they were up; and when they were down,
they were down;
and when they were only half-way up…

… they were in the 'space between' – in what we might term a 'liminal
space'. Neither up nor down, neither here nor there, betwixt and
between.

This book claims that most of life is lived in the 'space between'. Yet,
all too often, we can have a practical understanding of the Christian
life which hopes only to move 'from victory unto victory' and which
merely equips us to live in the certain and the secure. The good news
is that to live within the biblical story and the Christian tradition is to
have all the resources that we require for life where it is most often
located: amid disruption, uncertainty and a loss of momentum.

Caroline Welby writes that 'we tend to go through life without experiencing it in its fullness'.[3] It's like when you drive from A to B on a route that you are familiar with, and you get to the destination but can't remember exactly how you did it. All too often this is how we do life: on autopilot, as though we are sleepwalking our way through it. I often observe a stream of schoolchildren passing the front of our house on a weekday morning. Some are akin to walking zombies: heads down, eyes glued to phones, seemingly inattentive to the world around them. This inattentiveness to life is how I can live if I'm not careful. Sometimes, I merely follow the path of least resistance, the easiest way through. The focus of this book is the question of how God captures our attention to wake us up to the fullness of life. As I look back through my life so far, I reflect that in times and seasons of disruption, God has been at work to jolt me out of my slumber.

The Latin word *limina*, from which we get 'liminal', means 'threshold' – the place 'betwixt and between'. It's when we're out of our old comfort zone, and we're waiting in the dark, on the threshold of what comes next. It's when we've left the tried-and-tested, but have not yet been able to replace it with anything else. It's when our old world has come to an end, or worse still simply fallen apart, and we're left in limbo wondering what the new world may look like. There are countless examples of what liminal space might look like in practice, but they all carry with them the common characteristics of grief, confusion, ambiguity and loss of control, to name but a few. It's a hard place to be in because we each arrange our lives for the sake of predictability and control, comfort and security – and 'the space between' offers us none of these.

Getting stuck on 'the Way'

One of the earliest designations given to the community of those who followed Jesus was 'the Way', derived from the well-known statement by Jesus, 'I am the way and the truth and the life. No one comes to the Father except through me' (John 14:6). 'The Way' is used several times in the book of Acts: for example, when describing those believers whom Saul was opposed to before his Damascus Road experience; and then (now named Paul) his representation of 'the Way' in his missionary activities.[4]

'The Way' is a deep pastoral theme as well. It speaks of the 'journey' that is inherent to our discipleship – that dynamic relationship of following Jesus to which we are all invited. It captures a vital sense of motion and momentum. Following Jesus is never a guarantee of a comfortable life – it cannot be since 'the Way' in Mark's gospel is the journey towards Jerusalem and to Jesus' suffering and death on the cross. Equally, following Jesus is never meant to be something static. It should always take us onward as, led by the Spirit, we go ever deeper in our relationship with the Father.

Yet, despite this, there are undoubtedly times on that journey of discipleship when we seem to get 'stuck'. There are seasons when our experience of life appears to be taking us nowhere – or, if it is taking us anywhere, then it feels like it's downwards. It is precisely *these* times, these liminal seasons of life, that this book seeks to explore. They are the times and seasons – the spaces between – that we often want to hide from, and yet the very moments, I believe, that God is most able to use for his plans and purposes and, against all expectations, to lead us onward with him.

Mind the gap!

We enter a space between whenever we encounter disruption in our lives. Perhaps something changes unexpectedly, or crisis hits, or a season naturally comes to an end and there is a significant transition to make. There are endless external circumstances that might trigger a disruptive season in our lives: for example, a serious illness, the end of a close relationship, the death of a loved one, the loss of a job or income, or the failure of a longing to be realised. Even positive changes, full of new beginnings – such as getting married or having a baby, moving to a new place or starting a new job – can have within them an ending that needs to be faced. Sometimes the transition might be more developmental and constitute a slow, inner adjustment to a new perception of reality. These typically occur during adolescence, midlife or older age, but can equally take place anytime there is an inner awareness that the status quo is not satisfying and the search begins for an alternative. This inner feeling may, or may not, trigger an external change in the process.

In all of this, a 'VUCA' environment can ensue, in which the world is experienced as *volatile, uncertain, complex* and *ambiguous*.[5] For this reason, disruptive and liminal seasons are always experienced as places of pain. They are *volatile* in that something significant has changed, which destabilises us. They are *uncertain* in that we come to realise that life is no longer predictable. They are *complex* in that what has been familiar and certain is now lost, while the 'new normal' has not yet revealed itself. For all these reasons and more, they are deeply *ambiguous* and highly confusing.

Disruptive moments always involve loss and letting go. William Bridges describes five aspects of the natural 'ending' experience, which he terms 'the five dis's':

1 **Disengagement** – a separation from the contexts in which we have known or imagined ourselves. We disconnect either willingly or unwillingly from the activities, relationships, settings and roles that used to be of importance to us.

2 **Dismantling** – a taking apart of the structures that have sustained life for a time, whether they be our relationships, our sense of purpose, our rootedness in place, or our outlook on life. In a process of mourning, we stop thinking of ourselves as part of a 'we' and start thinking as an 'I'.

3 **Disidentification** – a loss of the old ways of defining ourselves. The end of a particular identity that once stemmed, perhaps, from a relationship, role or competency leaves us no longer quite sure who we are.

4 **Disenchantment** – a sense of being disappointed, let down, or disillusioned by someone, or something, that once held meaning or significance for us. This is the cost of the faith and trust that we exercise in different ways as inevitable parts of living.

5 **Disorientation** – a feeling of bewilderment and 'lostness', as vital parts of us slip away. All the customary signs of location are gone, and we cannot move forward into the future because we no longer know the way.[6]

Such endings create an inevitable emptiness. The old world has been relinquished, but there is not yet a new world to lay hold of. We are grieving a loss, yet are unable to define the shape of the hope into which we can step. The result is that we can sometimes fall down the gap that is the space between the two. Whenever I'm in London and I take the Tube, I'm relentlessly reminded to 'mind the gap between the train and the platform'. I can do this with ease. Unfortunately, however much I am reminded to 'mind the gap' between my endings and my beginnings, there is simply no avoiding these spaces between. In such spaces, there is only a void of nothingness which easily unsettles us. All our survival instincts are, naturally, to hurry back or to rush forwards. Yet, cruelly, we are unable to do either. There is no going back – things have happened which cannot be undone and which will leave their mark forever. Equally, there is no fast-forwarding through this time – we don't know where it will take us, so we can't anticipate the way ahead. We grope at something solid to lay hold of, but all we find are shadows that slip through our grasp.

To live well in the emptiness of the space between is a complex thing. The very sequence of an ending, a space between and a new beginning might not even happen in that order. For example, a new beginning, such as a new job in a new place, might trigger the realisation of a whole number of endings that are taking place and plunge a person into a space between. It may be a while before the new beginning can be fully embraced on the inside. Equally, someone in a relationship might sense an increasing disconnection from their partner and internally disengage long before any external ending comes about. These are confusing and ambiguous phases of life to process. We sometimes hope that there might be an easy fix for all of our problems – a switch that can be flipped to make things okay, or a few simple steps to bring about a happy ending. When a machine, such as a car, is broken, it isn't the whole car that goes through the process of travail. Instead, the faulty part is identified and either mended or a replacement part brought in. If only it could be the same for us.

Yet no simple solution exists for the pain of what we encounter in our losses and endings. There is no key, switch or fix that will do the job. Nonetheless, there is a power, I believe, to naming and framing the empty 'non-experiences' of our lives in the ways that this book will explore. This will not explain what is happening to us, but it can give us a renewed vision for confusing times. The lenses offered are not hard, literal and precise, for we are each unique and complex. No one can say to us, 'I know how you feel', for even where the externals might be similar, we all experience and process things in such radically different ways. Instead, the vision opened up is soft, meta-phorical and ambiguous. In this, I have found, both for myself and for others with whom I've conversed that there is strength to gain in realising that, though we *feel* lost, we are not lost. Instead, we are *somewhere* on the grid, even if we can't locate ourselves exactly. There is also encouragement in realising that our experiences, while unique, share a commonality with the stories of many others down the ages and within the present.

The origins of the term 'liminal'

'Liminality' emerges out of the field of anthropology. It describes the middle stage of rituals, as participants stand at the threshold between their previous way of structuring reality and the new way that the ritual establishes. This middle stage – this space between – is always marked by ambiguity and disorientation.

The concept of liminality was first developed in the early 20th century by folklorist Arnold van Gennep in his 1906 book, *The Rites of Passage*. Van Gennep claimed that all rites of passage followed a threefold sequence, composed of pre-liminal rites, liminal rites and post-liminal rites.[7] In pre-liminal rites (or *rites of separation*), there is a metaphorical death – something of the past that must be left behind. The middle stage of ambiguity and disorientation – that of liminal rites (or *transition rites*) – has two essential characteristics to it. First, the rite must follow a known sequence, and second, there must be a figure of authority presiding over it. The term 'liminality' was introduced to describe the passing through that marks the boundary between two phases of existence and reality. This middle stage is where the transition, albeit imprecisely, takes place. Post-liminal rites (or *rites of incorporation*) are then the stage in which the participant is reincorporated into society as a 'new' being with a new identity.

Victor Turner, who is considered to have rediscovered the importance of liminality, considered the initiation of children into adulthood to be the most typical rite. The awkwardness of teenage years, in which so much is up for grabs in terms of identity and belonging within family and community, is a classic example of the ambiguity and disorientation of the liminal middle stage. In the first phase, there must be a 'death' as childhood is left behind, while the crossing of the threshold leads to the celebration of a new adult and receiving them into society.

It is not difficult to see how baptism functions as the primary rite of passage within the Christian community, capturing each of the three stages in van Gennep's sequence. There is the death of the old person in the waters of baptism, giving birth to the new creation that arises out of the waters now that the threshold between death and new life has been crossed. This threshold, that liminal space, is located somewhere down in the font or baptistry.

Through the work of Turner, the concept of liminality began to be applied to a range of contexts beyond ritual passages in small-scale societies. More recently, usage of the term has broadened to describe political and cultural change as well.[8]

The importance of the disruptive moments in our lives

The space between is a place of great pain. At the same time, it is also a location of great opportunity and overwhelming hope, for in it we stand on the threshold of something altogether new. Vitally, disruption creates a unique space for reimagination. The emptiness of the space between offers a whole new perspective from which to glimpse life both as it was before and as it might be in the future. The space between, or, in Bridges' language, the 'neutral zone', 'provides access to an angle of vision on life that one can get nowhere else'.[9] This reimagination opens the door to the possibility of transformation. If the goal of the Christian life is to be transformed more and more into the image of Jesus Christ (2 Corinthians 3:18; Romans 8:29), then the disruptive seasons of life may be the most important means through which God accomplishes this. Importantly, *the disruptive process itself* is the source of renewal. This is to say that any change and transformation within us happens not *despite* what we perceive to be confusing, unsettling and even downright awful, but precisely *because of it* and only *through it*. The truth is that disruption and the liminal space that follows offer moments of intense creativity and profound opportunity for us. Richard Rohr comments:

> Nothing good or creative emerges from business as usual. This is why much of the work of God is to get people into liminal space, and to keep them there long enough so they can learn something essential. It is the ultimate teachable space... maybe the only one.[10]

It is sometimes only when we are betwixt and between, and hence out of control, that God has the opportunity to regain control and to mould our lives into the shape that he would have for us. Left to our own devices, we all too easily become 'comfortably numb', in the words of Pink Floyd. For this reason, Rohr describes God as 'the ultimate opportunist'. God certainly does not wish unhappiness upon us, though when those seasons come, he is uniquely able to redeem them for the sake of his eternal purposes. God can work *all things* together for the good of those who love him (Romans 8:28). It is for this reason that Elizabeth O'Connor, one of the founders of the Church of the Saviour in Washington DC, writes, 'Our chance to be healed comes when the waters of our life are disturbed.'[11] M. Scott Peck agrees:

> The truth is that our finest moments are most likely to occur when we are feeling deeply uncomfortable, unhappy, or unfulfilled. For it is only in such moments, propelled by our discomfort, that we are likely to step out of our ruts and start searching for different ways or truer answers.[12]

Rohr goes even further:

> Most spiritual giants try to live lives of 'chronic liminality' in some sense. They know it is the only position that ensures ongoing wisdom, broader perspective and ever-deeper compassion. The Jewish prophets... St Francis, Gandhi, and John the Baptist come to mind.

Yet most of us would not see ourselves as 'spiritual giants'. We would far rather choose predictability over uncertainty, control over chaos, the status quo over that which is unknown. We get locked into our tightly defined worlds, which we order so as to keep anything unpredictable or beyond our immediate control to a minimum. One unforeseen but inevitable consequence of such lifestyle arrangements is to define a place for God within our schemes, rather than letting him define one for us within his. In all of this, we are seeking to impose an artificial certainty on our lives. However, as Walter Brueggemann has rightly identified, certitude, though alluring, is ultimately powerless to deliver what we most desire:

We all have a hunger for certitude, and the problem is that the Gospel is not about certitude, it's about fidelity [faithfulness]. So what we all want to do if we can is immediately transpose fidelity into certitude, because fidelity is a relational category and certitude is a flat, mechanical category. So we have to acknowledge our thirst for certitude and then recognise that if you had all the certitudes in the world it would not make the quality of your life any better because what we must have is fidelity.[13]

Brueggemann reminds us that it is possible to seek *certitudes* in life apart from any relational proximity *to* God – even when those certitudes concern God himself! Yet to be *faithful* demands a quality of relationship, a walking with Christ through 'the thick and the thin' of life, an obedience to his call to 'follow me'. It is only in such an environment that he can hone the sense of identity that we carry; only in such a context that he can make us the people that he wants us to be, as he forms us more and more into the image of Christ. All of this can happen in the liminal seasons of life. Just as water finds itself in an in-between stage when it is either heated to become steam or cooled to become ice, there are plenty of in-between stages on 'the Way' in which we may not be exactly sure where we are or what is going on. However, as with water, what is of greatest importance is that transformation *is* taking place.

Ironically, the seasons in which we appear to get stuck can be the ones that change us the most. Those that seem to propel us downward can end up leading us onward. There are insights and perspectives that can only come in the space between, wherein 'death' gives birth to 'new life'. Victor Turner attributed an unequivocally positive connotation to liminal situations as a means of renewal. However, it must be realised that disruptive spaces do not automatically give way to uniformly positive consequences in our lives. Suffering doesn't *always* make good. Time is not *always* a healer. In the same way that bones can sometimes reset in all the wrong ways, so lives can sometimes 'reset' badly as well. There's a deep question of how we respond to all that life throws at us, and to the grace of God that works within us, which is the focus of the chapters ahead.

The diagram below aims to set out something of what is in process during times of disruption and liminality:

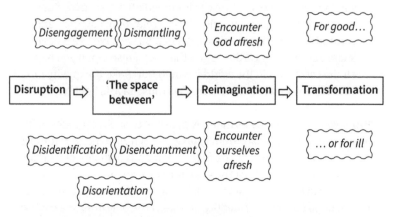

Summary of the book to come

In the preface to the 1982 edition of *Capitalism and Freedom*, Milton Friedman observed: 'Only a crisis – actual or perceived – produces real change. When that crisis occurs, the actions that are taken depend on the ideas that are lying around.' I believe that the living Christian tradition – the scriptures, the seasons of the church, our practices of prayer and our examples of faith – has plenty of ideas 'lying around' to help us live through our crises and liminal seasons. The challenge of the space between is to dig deeper into this treasure that lies all around us and which is freely available to us.

In the chapters that follow, we will explore all of this in more detail. We will begin with Jacob and two disruptive moments in his life that played a particular role in shaping him for God's purposes. We will then move on to explore five metaphors for the disruptive seasons of our lives: *the time of waiting* (when life is put on hold); *the place of exile* (when life feels alien); *the wilderness* (when life is stripped back); *the storm* (when life is shaken); and *the pit* (when life sinks to the bottom). These metaphors can give us a helpful way of framing our in-between moments in life – offering a vocabulary to connect with them, and holding out hope as we stand on the threshold and wait for chinks of light to appear around doors that seem to be closed.

It is vital to realise that these five metaphors neither signify a scheme to follow from start to finish, nor represent an ordered progression through our own disruptive and liminal experiences. Rather, they are each a different way of framing the same experiences. The aim is to offer several different lenses on to the ambiguity of the space between, so that hope may be found and resources drawn upon for the journey.[15] We might resonate with one, two or more of the metaphors in particular, but they are all different ways of speaking about the same thing. We all know that a diamond emerges from the rough and only finds its beauty through processes of cutting and polishing. In the same way, these liminal experiences offer those processes in our lives. Within the mysterious working of God, they form something beautiful in us – though it will seldom, if ever, feel this way at the time. The aim, then, will be to keep turning the diamond, to see what light is shed on these dark and difficult seasons. The ambiguity of liminality means that the more perspectives we can garner on them, the more we might be able to draw something from them.

In this, N.T. Wright's concept of worldview as being made up of *story*, *symbol*, *praxis* and *question* is helpful.[14] For each of the five metaphors of the space between, we will explore *story* through scripture – Old Testament, New Testament and supremely the life of Jesus – as well as the lives of Christian saints, both historical and contemporary. We will look at *praxis* – those ways in which we embed our beliefs – through the seasons of the church year as well as time-honoured Christian practices, bringing much-needed perspective and offering pathways for transformation. We will see the way in which the psalms, not least the psalms of disorientation, ask key *questions* of God and self in an effort to locate us again. In addition, questions for reflection are offered at the end of each chapter. We will explore all of this *symbolically* through the art of a friend whose pencil sketches run through the book and are explored in words on page 184. Yet, the true symbol for the space between is the cross of Jesus Christ. Living in the space between is so painful precisely because it is unavoidably a dying to self and a journey into the crucifixion of Christ. Each of the metaphors point to this, and we will explore Good Friday and Holy Saturday in more detail in chapters 6 and 7. However, what gives hope beyond anything else is that resurrection always comes in the wake of crucifixion. This means that, by the power of the Spirit, new life can always emerge from the tomb in which the old is being laid to rest.

Metaphor	Sacred time	Sacred practice
Time of waiting	Advent	Prayer
Place of exile	Epiphany	Pilgrimage
Wilderness	Lent	Fasting
Storm	Good Friday	Complaint
Pit	Holy Saturday	Silence

In all of this, my prayer is that strength may be found for those times in life when it so often fails, and that hope might be glimpsed of God strangely at work, even when he can seem to be so very far away.

Covid-19 as a space between

It has been interesting to write the bulk of this book during the Covid-19 pandemic. There has been a profound congruence between the topic of the book and the experience of Covid-19 and lockdown. I've noticed the way that people have intuitively framed their understanding of the pandemic through metaphor, including those that we explore in this book.

Usually, our experiences of the liminal seasons of life do not overlap. We go through them as separate individuals or smaller groups, siloed from the confusing in-betweens that others are experiencing. What feels almost unprecedented about Covid-19 is our global experiencing of a space between together.

At the time of this book's publication, we cannot know the full effects of Covid-19. In lockdown, we have imagined ways in which our home lives, patterns of work and gathering as churches may be affected in the long-term. We have seen the economic, social and environmental effects of lockdown and envisioned new futures for our world. We do not know exactly what the future will look like, but we know that it will be different. This experience has affected us all profoundly and the world has changed, perhaps forever. In this sense, as with all disruptive and liminal seasons of life, there may be no going back to normal – only forward into a new future.

Prayer – 'Disturb us, Lord'

Disturb us, Lord, when we are too well pleased with ourselves,
When our dreams have come true
Because we have dreamed too little,
When we arrived safely
Because we sailed too close to the shore.

Disturb us, Lord, when
With the abundance of things we possess
We have lost our thirst
For the waters of life;
Having fallen in love with life,
We have ceased to dream of eternity
And in our efforts to build a new earth,
We have allowed our vision
Of the new Heaven to dim.

Disturb us, Lord, to dare more boldly,
To venture on wider seas
Where storms will show your mastery;
Where losing sight of land,
We shall find the stars.
We ask You to push back

The horizons of our hopes;
And to push into the future
In strength, courage, hope, and love.
M.K.W. Heicher[16]

Questions for reflection

1 Do you characteristically see disruption as an inconvenience or an opportunity? Why do you think this might be?
2 What have been the main disruptions, or 'spaces between', in your life? Try to plot them on a timeline.
3 Pick one of those times and try to get 'inside' of it. How did (or does) it feel in terms of disengagement, dismantling, disidentification, disenchantment and disorientation?

2

Two disruptive moments in the life of Jacob

When Jacob awoke from his sleep, he thought, 'Surely the Lord is in this place, and I was not aware of it.'
GENESIS 22:16

The fawning etiquette of unctuous prayer is utterly foreign to the Bible. Biblical prayer is impertinent, persistent, shameless, indecorous. It is more like haggling in an outdoor bazaar than the polite monologues of the church.[1]
Walter Wink

God uses the unlikeliest of people. This is the consistent witness of the Bible, even in the most seminal moments of salvation history, as he works through characters such as Ruth, Esther, Peter and Paul. What's also true is that each of these named would only become who they were called to be through the disruptive seasons of their lives. Perhaps no one in the Old Testament exemplifies the potential of such disruptive seasons more than Jacob, the character from whom the people of Israel are named. The two most definitive and formative events in his life came when he found himself in a space between – one at a spot later called Bethel ('house of God'), and the other at a site later named Peniel ('face of God'). In neither was Jacob settled; rather he was 'on the way', in between places.

Jacob at Bethel (Genesis 28:10–22)

Background

Jacob and his elder brother, Esau, were part of the archetypal dysfunctional family – split down the middle with a father, Isaac, who favoured the elder son and a mother, Rebekah, whose affections lay with the younger. As they grew up, Esau was the alpha male – rough and rugged, hunting out in the open country, while Jacob was more of a mummy's boy, preferring to stay near to her side. The relationship between Jacob and Esau completely fell apart on two occasions when power was transferred from the elder to the younger, both of which were in exchange for food.

In the first, Esau returned from hunting one day feeling famished. Jacob meanwhile was cooking a stew. Any decent human being, not least in that culture, would have seen an opportunity for hospitality, but not Jacob. For Jacob, this was the opportunity for a power play: Esau's desperation for the 'red stuff' Jacob was cooking was something to exploit. As the elder son in a tribal society, Esau held the birthright, which gave him a position of leadership in the family and established his claim of a double share in the inheritance. This was something that Jacob had his eyes on. Esau traded the prestige of his future for survival in the present, but instantly knew he'd been done over. The resentment in him would only grow.

The second occasion to drive a chasm between the siblings came towards the end of their father's life. Aware that he did not have long left, Isaac prepared for the succession, which he naturally anticipated would benefit the elder son rather than the younger. Isaac commissioned Esau to prepare his favourite food for him – the provision of a meal constituted an essential part of the blessing ritual – yet he was unaware that his wife had overheard this and would turn the ceremony against his wishes. Rebekah was cool and calculating and issued instructions to Jacob, manipulating her intimate knowledge of her husband's tastes. She prepared Jacob to stand in for Esau, dressing him in his elder brother's clothes, and, in a farcical twist, even masking the smoothness of his skin with goatskin to make him resemble the hairy man that was Esau!

The pantomime scene played out, and, though the now-blind Isaac had alarm bells ringing in his ears regarding the soft voice of Jacob, he was taken in by the goatskin trick and the smell of Esau's clothes. Isaac pronounced the blessing, which could not be undone, even as the truth of what had happened was revealed. The opportunistic Jacob had struck again, more than ably assisted by his deceitful mother, and Esau could only pick up the scraps that were left. The younger son had truly lived up, or rather down, to his name – 'he grasps at the heel'. Meanwhile a broken Esau vowed that, when his father was finally out of the picture, he would have his revenge. Even here, though, Esau was without guile, as what he said 'to himself' soon found its way back to Rebekah. Once again, she left Jacob in no doubt as to what had to be done. This time, it was Jacob who had to act desperately to ensure his own survival.

Bethel

Against this backdrop, Jacob finds himself in a space between. Leaving the family home in Beersheba, he must flee to the unknown place of Haran – a journey of over 3,000 miles – to stay with family that he has surely never met. For anyone, this would be a daunting journey, a step into the unknown. For the smothered and mollycoddled Jacob, it must have been little short of terrifying. Far from all that is familiar, and with nothing tangible as yet to lay hold of, Jacob is caught in a liminal space. As so often when we ourselves are found in such a place, there was simply no other option available to him.

Very early in his epic journey, Jacob stops for the night. As the sun sets, Jacob drifts off to sleep, exhausted by the exertion and the emotion. In his dream, he sees a place of connection between heaven and earth, with angels going up and down between the two. He also hears the promises that God has made to his forefathers Abraham and Isaac being repeated to him: that he will be given a huge family who will be a blessing to all peoples on the earth, and that God's presence will be with him and will watch over him.

In the morning, Jacob awakes to realise that perhaps it wasn't a dream after all. Caught between leaving and arriving, between the end of the old day and the beginning of the new, Jacob's dream matches the liminality of the moment. This is the thing about liminal places: they are deeply ambiguous in nature and we are rarely certain what to make of them. 'Surely the Lord is in this place,' Jacob ponders, 'and I was not aware of it' (v. 16).

We often have preconceptions of what God's presence feels like. It can too easily be equated with the mountain-top experience, the 'liver shiver' or the peaceful contentedness that all is well. Yet, by itself, this would be to equate the presence of God only with the good times in life. What about the rest? So much of my own life feels painfully ordinary at the best of times, and downright messy, confused, even out of control at other times. Do I really believe that the God I worship is only a 'good-time God'?

The entrance to St Paul's Cathedral in London greets the visitor with the words that Jacob goes on to exclaim: 'This is none other than the house of God; this is the gate of heaven' (v. 17). We might expect to find God in such a place as St Paul's, built for the glory of God. Yet the hope of the Bethel story is that God can be found precisely in the places and moments that we might never expect to locate him. Jacob was barely 60 miles into a long, long journey away from the familiar before he found that he was enfolded within the powerful and protective presence of the God of his ancestors. God's presence is there with us too in the disruptive seasons of our lives – it's just that, like Jacob, we are often unaware of it. 'Surely the Lord is in this place,' we can say with confidence in the space between, 'and I was not aware of it.' Quite uniquely, these times can turn out to be none other than the house of God and the gate of heaven for us – if only we have the eyes of faith to see.

The fruit of this disruptive moment in Jacob's life is clear. Jacob claims for himself the presence and the protection of God and makes a personal promise that the Lord will be *his* God. This liminal moment in his life is uniquely transformative for Jacob and becomes something of a conversion experience for him as, for the first time, he owns the faith of his forefathers for himself. In the same way, our own experiences of the space between become crossroads moments for us. They tend either to bring us closer to God or to solidify our drift away from him. They rarely seem to leave us as we were before. No wonder Jacob chooses to mark this place as sacred, calling it Bethel (the 'house of God'), as he uses his makeshift pillow as a pillar and pours oil over it. These disruptive, liminal moments in our lives are true landmarks in our journey with God. They shake us out of business as usual and shape us, according to our response to the grace of God that is at work within us, into the people that we will become – for good or for ill. Even the most painful of moments in our lives can become 'Bethel' – the dwelling of God.

Jacob at Peniel (Genesis 32:22–32)

Background

A second disruptive event in the life of Jacob comes 20 years later. After his encounter with God at Bethel, Jacob journeyed on and was watering his flocks one day when he met a woman called Rachel. She turned out to be his uncle Laban's daughter and he asked his uncle if he could marry her. Jacob would work seven years hard graft for her hand, yet when the night came, he was given the elder daughter Leah in her place. The tables had been turned and the deceiver had himself been deceived! Jacob would have to work another seven years for Rachel to be given to him as well. Through Leah and Rachel, and their servants Zilpah and Bilhah, Jacob became the father of twelve sons and one daughter.

After the birth of Joseph, the eleventh of his offspring, Jacob asked to return to his homeland. Cutting a deal, and then fixing it to ensure that he came off best, Jacob parted with enormous wealth: large flocks, camels and donkeys, and female and male servants. The old Jacob was back! Laban's resentment at this would send Jacob again on the run; however, when Laban eventually caught up with him three days later, the two managed to reach a border agreement. Going on his way soon after, Jacob encountered angels of the Lord, which led him to exclaim, 'This is the camp of God!' The Lord's presence was with him again.

What provision God made for Jacob: the house of God at Bethel and now the camp of God at Mahanaim! In times of disruption and liminality, we can so often feel that we must have done something wrong, that somehow we deserve what we are now experiencing. There is, of course, a place for the discipline of the Lord, though, where this is given, it comes not as punishment, but correction, for 'the Lord disciplines those he loves, as a father the son he delights in' (Proverbs 3:12; compare Hebrews 12:6). It is a sign of his love for us, not his rejection of us. Yet what the Jacob story teaches us above everything is that the grace of God is overwhelming. Jacob is not deserving of such encounters at Bethel and Mahanaim, yet the Lord lavishes them upon him all the same. So it is for us: both in the good times and the bad, when we can see it and when we can't, we can have full assurance of God's love that is always for us, and his presence that will never leave us nor forsake us.

However, a sterner threat than Laban was now on its way to Jacob, as Jacob's past was finally catching up with him. As Jacob entered Edom on his way back home, he was stepping on to his elder brother Esau's turf, and news reached Jacob that Esau was coming to meet him with 4,000 men. In great fear and distress, Jacob divided those with him into two groups, thinking that at worst he might escape with half of his entourage. He also sent a significant gift ahead to Esau in the hope of appeasing him before their meeting. All Jacob could then do was to wait – for that which was unknown, but seemed inevitable.

Jacob wrestles the angel

The scene that unfolds next is one of the most enigmatic in all of scripture. Its context is vital. At night, Jacob takes his two wives, his two female servants and his eleven sons and crosses over the ford of the Jabbok. After he has dispatched them across the stream, he sends over all his possessions too. Then Jacob is alone. He has nothing and no one around him. Jacob is in a deserted place – everything is stripped away and he is left to his own thoughts as he contemplates the storm that will surely wreak its full havoc upon him. Seasons of liminality can so often be like this, stripping us right back to the bone. Yet hidden within the crisis, there can be an opportunity and a gift. New vistas can open up which provide fresh clarity and perspective. This enables things that once seemed so important to gain their proper place in an unexpected blessing of the liminal place. The feeling of being alone at times like this can be hard to shake – however, once again, Jacob is *not* alone.

A man wrestles with Jacob until daybreak. For all Jacob knows, grappling in the dark, it could have been Esau that he was fighting. When the man realises that he cannot overpower Jacob, he strikes the socket of Jacob's hip, wrenching the hip from it. Jacob, who has been running hard from his past for so long, is finally forced to a halt as he is crippled. The man insists that Jacob let him go, but Jacob will not do so until he receives a blessing. The man pronounces on Jacob a new identity – Israel – for Jacob has struggled with God and with people. Just as at Bethel, Jacob becomes aware of the liminality and the ambiguity of the moment, as he realises that he has not simply been wrestling with a man, nor even with an angel. In the space between, things are seldom as they first seem. Instead, in some indescribable way, Jacob has been wrestling with *God*. He names the place accordingly – 'Peniel', meaning 'face of God' – for he has seen God face-to-face and has lived to tell the tale. The 'house of God', the 'camp of God', and now the 'face of God': God makes himself known to us when we least expect it. What divine wisdom and discernment we need to be aware of the existence and experience of such moments.

This second story of Jacob has so much to teach us about how to live within the disruptive and liminal moments of our lives. Three words will help us to unpack this: 'wrestling', 'wounds' and 'identity'.

Wrestling – praying in disruptive seasons

We all carry different 'working images' of God that shape how we relate to him. Without realising it, these often stem from other relationships in our lives or from fears we harbour as to what God really thinks of us, which we then project unconsciously on to our human-divine relationship. A.W. Tozer once said: 'What comes into our minds when we think about God is the most important thing about us.'[2] When times are hard, or we know we've made mistakes, we can sometimes think that God is 'out to get us' – as though the God we worship is 'tit-for-tat' and gives us what we deserve. In times of feeling more the absence than the presence of God, we might see God as a distant authority figure, removed from the situations that we are going through and uncaring. By the Holy Spirit at work within us, we need to know God as Jesus knew him: neither monstrous figure nor distant deity, but *abba*, Father – a God from whose love we can never be separated. I always thought I knew this, and in lots of ways I did, but I now see that this revelation hasn't always filtered through in its entirety.

All too often my default position towards God, whether through my own misconceptions or by learned behaviour, has been one of polite deference. An older lady in our congregation said to me during the first Covid lockdown, 'Well, I don't like what's going on, but we can't challenge him [God]. We just need to get on with it.' I recognise this same stoic passivity in my own dealings with God at times, as though I am only invited into a relationship of distant politeness. I am challenged by the insight of Walter Wink, who observes that such relatedness is foreign to the Bible; instead, he argues that 'biblical prayer is impertinent, persistent, shameless, indecorous. It is more like haggling in an outdoor bazaar than the polite monologues of the church.' The encounter of Jacob with God at Peniel takes us into this way of engaging with the divine. Jacob's wrestling with God is a wonderful parable of what authentic prayer should always look like. E.M. Bounds says that 'prayer in its highest form and grandest success assumes the attitude of a wrestler with God'.

My sense is that it has been in the disruptive and liminal seasons of my life that God has begun to teach me the beginnings of this way of relating to him. In these in-between spaces, I have learned not to be quite so polite in prayer. Perhaps it is that these circumstances, in the grace of God, have forced that politeness out of me. At these times, my prayer has become marked by something more akin to desperation, and in that desperation I have found myself far less willing to take everything lying down. Only now do I realise that this is how I should have been praying all along, because I'm convinced from this story in the life of Jacob that God is more than up for the fight. Wrestling is sweaty, indiscrete, unrespectable, but above all else it is intimate. Intimacy is what God craves from us above everything, and it is what we most need from him. God is like Jacob, ever the opportunist, and he uses these liminal moments in our lives to bring us up close and personal with him. In this fight, winning and losing pale into insignificance as, more than anything, we win God and he wins us.

Wounds – marked by disruptive seasons
When it becomes clear that Jacob cannot be overcome, God strikes him in the hollow of the thigh with a blow that must have been severe. The picture is painted of Jacob limping down the road towards the promised land, as the sun rises over a new day. It is a deeply poignant one. Jacob moves on towards his destination, yet he has been permanently marked by this struggle with God. Vitally, though, his wound speaks not of defeat and failure, but of hope and a future. Jacob has struggled and he has prevailed. His limp tells pervasively of the graciousness of God, who has preserved Jacob's life in the midst of the struggle and will continue to do so for the rest of his days.

It was the same for Jesus Christ, the one who became Israel for the sake of Israel and for the world. It has long fascinated me that Jesus Christ, the new Jacob, did not emerge from the tomb wound-free.

Instead, as he appeared to Thomas and the other disciples in the upper room, he bore scars on his body wrought by the nails with which he had been crucified and the spear with which he had been pierced. Yet, in the light of the resurrection, those wounds had been transfigured to speak not of defeat but of victory, not of failure but of glory. Supremely, they spoke – and still speak today – of the healing love and grace of God.

By the death and resurrection of Jesus Christ, it can be the same with *our* wounds. We will always be marked by the disruptive seasons through which we travel. The wounds left by these experiences may always remain with us, for it is rarely possible to emerge pristine and unscarred from such times. Miraculously, though, the testimony borne by these wounds can be that of hope and not despair, of triumph and not defeat. It is always possible for some wounds to fester, unhealed; yet the wounds that come from wrestling with God are able to speak a better word. The Japanese art of kintsugi, or kintsukuroi, illustrates this powerfully. It is the art of repairing pottery with gold, in the understanding that the piece is more beautiful for having been broken. In the gracious economy of God, it can be the same for us.

Identity – shaped within disruptive seasons

We often locate our identity in all the wrong places. The space between reveals where we have placed our security and certainty, our trust and our dependency, and how this warps our true sense of identity. In this space, we find the opportunity to reimagine not only something more of God but also something more of ourselves – who we are and who we are called to be. We receive the gift of our identity in Christ and the profundity of his revelation of who we truly are.

Jacob's wrestling with God transformed his identity forever. 'Jacob' meant 'supplanter', or 'he grasps at the heel'. It denoted the worst of who Jacob was: his strategising and scheming to get one over on another. It reminded him of his past – a past of which he was surely ashamed and to which he perhaps felt enslaved, never quite knowing how to change the script. Yet God's imagination for Jacob was so much more creative than this. In contrast, 'Israel' denoted one 'who prevails with God'. It signified Jacob at his best: wrestling with God, and winning. The new name saw a fresh start for him – the old was gone and the new had come (2 Corinthians 5:17) – a fresh start that was marked by a new and radical intimacy with God.

It's interesting to observe that Jacob asked the angel for his name but that this request was not granted. In ancient times, to know the true name of someone was to have authority over them. God remains elusive according to this story. He is for us, and he loves us, yet he won't be boxed in or tied down by us. He will be whatever he will be.[3] He has an authority over us that we don't have over him – this is not a relationship of equals. Nonetheless, we can be confident that God is at work within the disruptive seasons of our lives to shape us ever more into the identity that he has for us: the image and likeness of the person of Jesus Christ. God is longing that we relinquish control of our lives for long enough that, by his Spirit, he is able to transform our worst into his best. Every liminal moment of our lives can be a conversion experience for us: either for the first time or for the umpteenth time. God is a potter, continually forming us like clay through the toughest of experiences. He's a sculptor who uses the hard times to knock off our rough edges and to smooth out the masterpiece that he is creating in us. He's a painter who is painting a work of majestic art with our lives.

The story is told of a young artist who won an award for a painting of unusual merit. On receiving the award, he said to a friend, 'That really isn't my best painting.' 'Oh,' said the friend, 'then why didn't you exhibit your best?' With a smile he replied, 'Because my best painting is yet to be done.' So it is with us. God's best painting of us is always still to come, as we allow his grace to continue its work in us, not least through the disruptive and liminal seasons of our lives.

We turn now to the first of our lenses through which we can view such seasons – the time of waiting, or when life is put on hold.

Prayer of abandonment

Father,
I abandon myself into your hands; do with me what you will.
Whatever you may do, I thank you:
I am ready for all, I accept all.
Let only your will be done in me, and in all your creatures.
I wish no more than this, O Lord.
Into your hands I commend my soul;
I offer it to you
with all the love of my heart,
for I love you, Lord,
and so need to give myself,
to surrender myself into your hands,
without reserve,
and with boundless confidence,
for you are my Father.
Charles de Foucauld

Questions for reflection

1 Have you known any 'Bethel' encounters with God in any of your experiences of disruption and liminality?
2 In what ways have times of disruption and liminality changed the way that you have prayed or related to God?
3 What wounds do you still carry from those times? How do you see them now?

3

The time of waiting: when life is put on hold

I waited patiently for the Lord; he turned to me and heard my cry.
PSALM 40:1

If you're truly waiting on God, then you won't miss anything.
Louie Giglio

Human emotions – disappointment and frustration

'As Slow as Possible' is a keyboard work written by John Cage in the mid-1980s. The score consists of eight pages of music to be played at the piano or organ in the manner the title suggests. However, with no tempo marking in the original score, it is left to the interpreter to decide what 'as slow as possible' actually looks like in practice. In 2001, an ambitious group of artists with a lot of time on their hands began playing at a specially built organ at St Burchardi Church in Halberstadt, Germany. Their interpretation of 'As Slow as Possible' has a scheduled duration of 639 years, ending in the year 2640!

It can sometimes feel as though God, the artist, takes 'as slow as possible' to its absolute limits as we wait in the space between.

Why…? How long…?

These are the cries of many a human heart in turmoil. The first cry speaks of the incomprehension of hurt and suffering, something which takes place without any apparent reason. The second vocalises an enduring sense of agony and affliction. This isn't a one-off event, as awful as that would be, but a situation that is dragging on without end, closure or resolution; an agonised delay to justice and the making right of something.

Such cries are the natural exclamation of the human heart. They are precognitive and have to be uttered and exclaimed. They are the overflow of sentiments that can no longer be held within. Sometimes they have no clear direction – they are simply sent out into the ether – while at other times, they are directed towards a specific target. This may be a person or group, who are perceived as the source of what has gone wrong, or perhaps the community around, that they might shed some light on what is taking place. Ultimately, these cries are directed to God, and this is where they feel their greatest tension.

If God is so powerful and almighty, and also so loving and compassionate, then why do these things happen? Why are they permitted to endure? The world is in motion around us, yet we are stuck at a red light, unmoving. Everyone else in the waiting room has been seen by the physician, but no one is calling our name and we're unsure when, or even if, we'll ever be attended to. It's what Paul Scanlon, in his powerful sermon on the topic, calls the 'agony of divine delay'.[1]

The agony is so painful precisely because it appears divine in origin – in short, we expected better of God. This doesn't seem unreasonable. After all, if a friend failed so regularly to turn up when we asked to get together, or so consistently neglected to respond to our most urgent of needs, they likely wouldn't remain our friend for long. So why is God any different? Why is his timing so out? Why is he so poor at responding to the most obvious of signals? With a friend like this… It's all too easy to hear the mantra 'God has perfect timing', but when you're stuck in the agony of divine delay, such sentiment can feel shallow. Truth – even the most biblical sort – can seem painfully glib. There's a reason for this. The liminal space, the space between, only finds its significance in relation to what sits either side of it – the event and the resolution. A middle, by its very nature, must have something before and after it. All too often, people speak into our nothingness from a place of completion. Yet, life is not lived with the benefit of hindsight, and those going through a middle can have no idea of what they will step into next.

In the sections that follow, we will explore the resources of scripture and the Christian faith for living in a time of waiting – its stories and practices. These stories include the waiting of Abraham and Sarah, the waiting of Elizabeth, Zechariah, Mary, Simeon and Anna, and the waiting of Jesus Christ himself. They also take in the waiting of Nelson Mandela as well as that of a friend of mine. The practices of waiting include the imbibing of Psalm 130, the practice of the season of Advent and the practice of prayer.

Sacred scriptures

Old Testament – Abraham and Sarah

It's been said that if God makes you wait, you're in good company. Many of the heroes of the Old Testament had to wait – Joseph for 13 years, Moses for 40, Hannah for an unspecified length of time. One of the definitive examples of waiting in the Old Testament is that of Abraham – held up by Paul as the father of faith (Romans 4:11–12) – and his wife, Sarah.

The whole of Abraham's life can be summed up like this:

God says, 'I want you to leave your country, your people and your father's household.' Abraham asks, 'Where shall I go?' God replies, 'I'll tell you later. Just go.'

God says, 'I'll bring you to a new land.' Abraham asks, 'Where is it?' God replies, 'I'll tell you later. Just wander.'

God says, 'I'll give you a child and make you into a great nation.' Abraham asks, 'How?' God replies, 'I'll tell you later. Just wait.'

Abraham's is a life kept on hold; a life of waiting.

We first meet Abraham, or Abram as he is originally called, in Genesis 12. God calls him to leave his country, his people and his father's household (more of this in chapter 4), as God will provide him with a land and make him into a great nation for the blessing of many. Abram is 75 years old when this promise comes. He and his wife, Sarai (later Sarah), are childless and their biological clocks have certainly ticked on well by this stage. However, they will still be made to wait.

Around a decade later, God makes a covenant with Abram (Genesis 15). Abram has grown wealthy but is conscious that he does not have any offspring, such that his servant Eliezer of Damascus would inherit from him. God promises Abram that he will have a son of his own, and Abram believes the Lord and does not question that the promise will be fulfilled. Yet still he is made to wait.

More than a decade passes again before the promise is confirmed with the assurance that Sarah will have a son in a year's time (Genesis 18). Sarah hears this and laughs at the farce of the whole situation – Abraham is a year short of 100 and Sarah is long past the age of bearing children at nearly 90! However, sure enough, the promise of God is good and a few chapters later, in Genesis 21, a son, Isaac, is born to Abraham and Sarah. His name, 'he laughs', plays on Sarah's response to the ludicrous promise and the reality of God's fulfilling it. The father and mother of faith receive a son on account of the sheer grace and power of God. For truly, nothing is too hard for the Lord (Genesis 18:14).

It comes as a relief to realise that a crucial part of the story is missing here: the reality of human struggle. Waiting is hard, doing nothing is difficult. We all feel frustration when life is put on hold. None of us can sit on our hands for long. Ideas form in our minds, and we feel the need to help God out, just in case he has run out of ideas for a solution of his own. This is true of all of us, and it was also true of Abraham and Sarah.

Abraham's first offer of help to God was the suggestion that God must have had in mind for his servant, Eliezer, to come into his inheritance. Abraham adapts and adjusts God's promise to fit the current circumstances, such that a scaled-down version is produced. When God assures them that this isn't the case, Abraham and Sarah move on to their Plan B. Sarah sees a way of providing an heir by giving her slave-girl, Hagar, to Abraham. Abraham agrees to the plan. The consequences are disastrous for all involved.

It is hard to trust and it is difficult to wait.

My wife Sarah and I are grateful to have children of our own. However, we did face a time of waiting before conceiving our first child, which in that season felt like an eternity. Each month went by, we did the tests, and the results were crushingly negative. It seemed as though all of our friends were conceiving with remarkable ease, but it just wasn't happening for us. The script that we had written for our lives, and assumed that God would happily sign off on, was not being played out in reality.

In the middle of this season, Sarah's boss suggested we take some time out to visit Lindisfarne, also known as Holy Island. I will share more of this in the next chapter, but those few days were truly life-transforming for us. We knew God in a way that we had never known him before. The weakness and vulnerability of the circumstance bred in us a desperation for something, anything. It meant we were free to let God in, in ways that, had life been on the course we had set, we simply wouldn't have. We had to relinquish the possibility of having children and to embrace the promise of God still loving us and sustaining us in our lives together. In the pain of waiting and the agony of divine delay, we found God in the space between.

Introduction to lament

We will come to the practice of complaint in chapter 6, but something needs to be said here about the 'lament psalms' as they are key to the book of Psalms as a whole, as well as to the navigation of the space between. Though much has been written about them over the past generation or so, they remain neglected at a devotional level, yet without them we are poorly equipped for our journey.

Popular use of the Psalms can sometimes be reserved for those that assure, affirm and strengthen – including wonderful psalms such as Psalm 23, Psalm 91 and Psalm 103. However, the Psalms have even more to offer us than this. The writer who has most helped me to appreciate this is Walter Brueggemann.[2] Brueggemann divides the Psalms into psalms of 'orientation', 'disorientation' and 'new orientation' – matching the different seasons of our life and faith. 'Psalms of orientation' celebrate the joy, goodness and reliability of God, creation and God's law. 'Psalms of disorientation' fit those seasons of pain, suffering and death when we feel self-pity, resentment and rage. 'Psalms of new orientation' speak into the times when God does a new thing to bring coherence again. Such a way of viewing the psalms fits well with the Church of England's Tragedy and Congregations project, which encourages the cultivation of what it calls 'three-lensed seeing' – the capacity to contemplate events in the light of creation, the cross and the promise of a life from which every tear has been wiped away.[3]

Within Brueggemann's scheme, there are two primary movements – first, out of a settled 'orientation' into a season of 'disorientation' and second, from 'disorientation' into a 'new orientation'. That first movement describes the entire theme of this book, even as we find ourselves longing for the second to arrive. Brueggemann notes:

> This move is experienced partly as change to circumstance, but it is much more a personal awareness and acknowledgement of the changed circumstance. This may be an abrupt or a slowly dawning acknowledgement. It constitutes a dismantling of the old, known world and a relinquishment of safe, reliable

confidence in God's good creation. The movement of dismant-ling includes a rush of negativities, including rage, resentment, guilt, shame, isolation, despair, hatred and hostility.[4]

Walter Brueggemann has been particularly instrumental in call-ing attention to the value of lament in general and to the psalms of lament in particular. His article, 'The costly loss of lament', argues that, despite the great value of the psalms of lament, they are now virtually ignored by the church, meaning that lament itself is absent from both life and liturgy.[5] He notes the cost of this in terms of the loss of genuine covenant interaction, in which we can only be 'yes-men and women' before God – forfeiting the ability to wrestle with God in prayer that we reflected on earlier. He argues that the stifling of questions around the problem of pain, suffering and evil means that 'most contemporary prayer is denial, as though our secrets can be hid from God'.[6] Further-more, he insists, by not using the psalms of lament in the church, 'we have communicated two messages to people: either you must not feel that way (angry with God, for example) or, if you feel that way, you must do something about it somewhere else – but not here'.[7]

Vitally, lament gives permission to insist at least four things before God:[8]

1 Things are not right in the present arrangement.
2 They need not stay this way and can be changed.
3 The speaker will not accept them in this way, for the present arrangement is intolerable.
4 It is God's obligation to change things.

Furthermore, as Scott Ellington writes:

Biblical lament, while it does include tears, complaints and protests, is something more. It is the experience of loss suffered within the context of relatedness. A relationship of trust, inti-macy, and love is a necessary precondition for genuine lament. When the biblical writers lament, they do so from within the context of a foundational relationship that binds together the individual with members of the community of faith and that community with their God.[9]

So we may lose *certainty* in these seasons, but it is relational *fidelity* that is the greater priority. Such relatedness is the foundation to biblical lament and includes not only our relationship with God but also those with our sisters and brothers in the family of faith. We cannot hope to journey through the space between by ourselves, and we will need to express lament together with those closest to us. As we will see in chapter 7, Job, to his great cost, had friends who were unable to do this with him.

Psalm 130

Psalm 130 is a psalm of disorientation and waiting, one of the 15 songs of ascents (Psalms 120—134) that were sung by the Jewish pilgrims as they journeyed to Jerusalem and as they ascended Mount Zion to worship at the ancient temple.[10] The fact that the psalm begins with a 'cry' suggests that it should be classified as a lament – a request for God's help – however, it is a particular type of lament psalm in that it is a plea for pardon and forgiveness.[11]

The psalmist finds themself 'in the depths'.[12] This suggests a place where one is overwhelmed by suffering and oppression, not merely emotionally but physically and materially. Often this reality might come through no fault of our own; however, in this psalm the psalmist acknowledges that it is of their own making. In this place, they are unable to say to God, 'You must rescue me – I don't deserve this.' All they can do is appeal to God's mercy and grace.

The psalm can be divided into four sections of two verses each, which many modern translations observe in how the verses are set out. Another way of looking at the psalm is to see the structure in which, following the cry of verses 1–2, verses 3–8 explore sin (v. 3), then grace (v. 4), then expectation at the centre (vv. 5–7a), before parallel sections on grace (v. 7b) and sin (v. 8) conclude. This ancient device of chiasm served to focus the reader's attention on the centre of the psalm, which in this psalm is a waiting in hope. Psalms 130 and 131 use the verbs 'expect' and 'wait' five times, and near the end each issue commands to 'wait for the Lord'.

Like other lament psalms, Psalm 130 begins with a direct address to God – 'Out of the depths I cry to you, Lord' (v. 1). Some psalms speak *about* God, but lament psalms speak *to* God. Everything felt and experienced is directed in this way in the expectation that God will hear and be attentive (v. 2). In this way there is an acknowledgement of the absence of God in the experience of the psalmist at this moment. Something needs to change here. Specifically, there is a cry for mercy and pardon.

The following section (vv. 3–4) develops this and acknowledges the extent of human sin, which the psalmist confesses for themself. Nonetheless, there is the hope of standing before God and of serving him, because he is the source of forgiveness. If God kept a long list of sin, then there would be no hope for any of us, but he doesn't. Instead, our sin is erased, wiped out in his mercy and grace.

As a result, we come to the centre of the psalm, which consists of expectant waiting. Although lament is a record of suffering and a plea for help, it is also an act of hope. The theme of the centre is communicated through two related terms, 'to wait' and 'to hope', and each of these terms is found twice in verses 5–7. Such waiting, though, is not passive and it is not disconnected from that for which the psalmist waits. This waiting is urgent, even impatient.[13] Furthermore, it is not simply an attitude of hope that something, somehow, will happen. Instead, it is hope placed in a definitive object – here, the Lord, on whom the confidence of the psalmist rests. As a result, the psalmist emphasises the involvement of their 'whole being' in this intense process of waiting. Finally, the psalmist is also notably not 'empty' in the process of waiting. Instead, their waiting is filled with the abundance of God's word, his promise, which the psalmist is holding on to and which is sustaining them in hope.

The anticipation and longing of the psalmist is symbolised in verse 6 by a comparison with the guards who keep watch upon the city walls each night. The guards' hope is that they might pass the night successfully without threat or incident; therefore, they long for the coming of the morning, when they can finally breathe a sigh of relief. The psalmist, however, longs for the Lord even more than the watchmen long for the coming of the new day. There is also the sense that, as sure as comes the morning, so certain is the hope that God will hear the prayer of the psalmist even as they wait in the space between.

Lament psalms often make a transition from prayer to praise, but here the transition is from lament to exhortation. The final two verses are addressed to the wider community of faith, which is encouraged to follow the example of the psalmist and to 'hope in the Lord'. This upbeat finish is accentuated with an abandonment of the three-times repeated alternation from 'Yahweh' to 'Adonai' (vv. 1–2, 3, and 5–6). Instead in verse 7, 'Yahweh' is repeated, as a poetic climax that emphasises the importance of that name. There are two reasons for this hope for Israel. First, with Yahweh there is deep covenant commitment – 'unfailing love'. Second, there is the promise of abundant rescue – 'full redemption'. This speaks to Israel's communal memory as the covenant people of God, wherein those memories generate deep affective responses of love, gratitude and hope, based upon God's faithfulness in the past.

The final verse answers the rhetorical question posed in verse 3. This confirms the assertion of Brueggemann that 'when YHWH is rightly understood, sin from the outset is penultimate at best. What is ultimate is the mercy of YHWH that outflanks human failure.'[14]

New Testament – Zechariah, Elizabeth, Mary, Simeon and Anna (Luke 1—2)

We find a number of people waiting in the opening chapters of Luke's gospel: Zechariah, Elizabeth, Mary, Simeon and Anna, who are representatives of a waiting Israel. The psalms, as we have just seen in Psalm 130, are full of admonitions to wait:

I remain confident of this: I will see the goodness of the Lord in the land of the living. Wait for the Lord; be strong and take heart and wait for the Lord.
PSALM 27:13–14

We wait in hope for the Lord; he is our help and our shield. In him our hearts rejoice, for we trust in his holy name. May your unfailing love be with us, Lord, even as we put our hope in you.
PSALM 33:20–22

Hope in the Lord and keep his way. He will exalt you to inherit the land; when the wicked are destroyed, you will see it.
PSALM 37:34

Zechariah, Elizabeth, Mary, Simeon and Anna remind us of the power of waiting with others in the space between. This is what the writer of Ecclesiastes understood:

Two are better than one, because they have a good return for their labour: if either of them falls down, one can help the other up. But pity anyone who falls and has no one to help them up.
ECCLESIASTES 4:9–10

One of the many paradoxes of this middle-time is that we find ourselves in desperate need both of our own space in silence and solitude and the loving and supportive community of others around us. Here, the latter is stressed as we see the power of community to hold and encourage for the long wait. The temptation for others is for them to try to fix and make right, to offer 'answers' and 'solutions'. In Luke 1—2, there is a more powerful model of those who share a common vision waiting in the void together.

Henri Nouwen has spoken and written beautifully on the spirituality of waiting.[15] He makes a number of brilliant observations.

First, spiritual waiting is not an empty experience. We might assume that the waiting room is a 'nothing space' in which we are looking to receive something. However, Nouwen reminds us that 'people who wait have received a promise that allows them to wait'. Zechariah was given the promise that Elizabeth would bear him a son (Luke 1:13). Mary was given the promise that she would give birth to a son (Luke 1:31). What promises might God have given to us? Such promises are like seeds which take root in us and begin to grow. Nouwen observes that 'we can only really wait if what we are waiting for has already begun for us. So waiting is never a movement from nothing to something. It is always a movement from something to something more.' Our waiting is filled with the hope that comes from the abundant promises of God. Waiting is nurturing the moment and is always full, rather than empty, as an experience.

Second, spiritual waiting is not a passive experience. It is not akin to the experience of waiting for a bus that is late, about which we can do nothing, which leaves us with no alternative than to sit back and 'wait'. On the contrary, Nouwen observes from scripture that 'those who are waiting are waiting very actively'. They are leaning in, not sitting back. This follows from the previous point that those waiting know there is something in the soil of their hearts that is growing in secret. Nouwen says, 'Active waiting means to be fully present to the moment, in the conviction that something is happening where you are and that you want to be present to it.' This calls for great patience, of course. Nouwen notes that 'impatient people are always expecting the real thing to happen somewhere else… but patient people dare to stay where they are'. Isaiah 40:31 says that 'those who hope in the Lord will renew their strength'. Fascinatingly, the Brown-Driver-Briggs lexicon points out that this word describes the work of a spider in building a web. When a spider threads a web, it does so in the expectation that something good will land in it. It doesn't run around chasing things; rather, it waits. Yet, the waiting is not passive, it is active in that a web to catch good things must be threaded together. There is a leaning in to the future, rather than a sitting back in the present.

Third, spiritual waiting is not about our wants and wishes – it is about waiting for something bigger and more open-ended than this. The spider doesn't know quite what will land in its web, but it waits open-endedly to receive something that is good. Nouwen observes that we tend to wait for something highly specific, which we have moulded and shaped according to our own desires. In this way, our waiting is actually a way of controlling the future, of saying to God, 'This is the way the future *must* turn out!' In this dynamic, we become God and God becomes merely the fulfiller of the transactions that we desire. However, spiritual waiting is always open-ended and energised by hope. As Nouwen writes, 'Hope is trusting that something will be fulfilled, but fulfilled according to the promises and not just according to our wishes. Therefore, hope is always open-ended.' This takes a radical releasing of control on our part – an opening of our imaginations to the vast imagination of God, trusting that his ways are higher than our ways and his thoughts than our thoughts (Isaiah 55:9).

Jesus Christ – his first 30 years

Jesus Christ knew what it was to wait. If we find ourselves in a place of waiting, we're not only in good company, we're in the best of it. The agony of divine delay would be experienced by Jesus most achingly upon the cross and within the tomb. Yet Jesus had learned to wait on God long before this. Extraordinary as it is to think about, Jesus had to wait around 30 years in his life before his ministry went public. Such waiting was a hidden experience, and it is striking given the importance of the man how little we know about the vast majority of Jesus' life on earth. The gospels of Matthew and Luke celebrate Jesus' birth in different ways, but there is then a significant gap before the beginning of Jesus' public ministry when he was 'about thirty years old' (Luke 3:23).

After Jesus' birth, Matthew's gospel tells us about the visit from Magi (pagan astrologers from the east; Matthew 2:1–12), the family's flight for refuge in Egypt (Matthew 2:13–18) and their eventual return after the death of Herod (Matthew 2:19–23). Matthew's gospel then jumps ahead to the ministry of John the Baptist, who prepares the way, with

Jesus as a fully grown adult. There is nothing at all about the intervening 30-plus years of childhood, adolescence and early adulthood.

Luke's gospel has more to say than Matthew's, yet it still summarises three decades of the most important life in human history in surprisingly limited terms. Luke tells of the angel's announcement to the shepherds (Luke 2:8–21) and the young family's first visit to the temple, where they encounter Simeon and Anna (Luke 2:22–38). Twelve years of the paradigmatic human life are then captured in just one sentence: 'The child grew and became strong; he was filled with wisdom, and the grace of God was on him' (Luke 2:40). The story of Jesus impressing all at the temple at the age of twelve is described (Luke 2:41–51), before two decades of living are summed up in another simple sentence: 'And Jesus grew in wisdom and stature, and in favour with God and man' (Luke 2:52).

Given the impact of Jesus' life, we might find it astonishing that so little is known about his childhood, adolescence and early adulthood. I once read a story in which a mother was asking her son to tidy his bedroom. 'What would Jesus do?' she asked. 'He'd have zapped it tidy,' came the reply. Like this boy, we might fill the lack of space regarding Jesus' formative years with all sorts of speculative imaginings about what Jesus did and what he was like. Yet, surely the space between in the account of Jesus' life speaks a word of hope to us regarding our own seasons of waiting.

Surely it dignifies the places of obscurity and seasons of painfully ordinary human existence that we ourselves live through. If these are good enough for the Son of God, then why not for us? Does it not also offer an alternative perspective on our own incessant need to be productive in every moment? Given that Jesus lived just a little over 30 years, my plan, had I been in charge of cosmic salvation, would have been to put a much higher percentage of such limited time into public ministry. God made it count for less than 10% of Jesus' life. It seems that God's maths – his sense of what is productive – is markedly different from my own.

Instead, in these 'wasted' years, Jesus walked the ordinary, unglamorous path of basic human growth and development. He grew physically, in a body just like ours, with all the growing pains that this would involve. He grew in wisdom – there was not a divine download of this given to him at birth, but rather an accumulation of knowledge was gained by learning how to live well in God's world over time. Similarly, he grew in obedience to both earthly (Luke 2:51) and divine authority. In particular, and consistent with a central focus of this book, Jesus learned obedience in his suffering, and through this he was made complete (Hebrews 5:7–9). In all of this, Jesus grew in favour with God and with those around him. The goal of our lives is to be complete in our love of God and our love of neighbour. Even for Jesus, this could only take place in the obscurity of waiting in the space between.

Sacred time – Advent

Advent is the season in which the church waits. On one level, this is a waiting to celebrate the coming of the Christ-child at Christmas. However, on an eschatological level, it is a waiting for the coming again of Christ to repair the universe, to renew all things and to wipe away every tear from our eyes (Revelation 21:4).

The story is told of the contrasting responses of a father and a mother to the sadness of their child:

> One December afternoon, a group of parents stood in the lobby of a nursery school waiting to claim their children after the last pre-Christmas class. As the youngsters ran from their lockers, each one carried in their hands the 'surprise', the brightly wrapped package on which they had been working diligently for weeks.
>
> One small boy, trying to run, put on his coat and wave to his parents all at the same time, slipped and fell. The 'surprise' flew from his grasp, landed on the floor and broke with an obvious ceramic crash.

The child began to cry inconsolably. His father, trying to minimise the incident and comfort the boy, patted his head and murmured, 'Now, that's all right, son. It doesn't matter. It really doesn't matter at all.'

But the child's mother, somewhat wiser in such situations, swept the boy into her arms and said, 'Oh, but it does matter. It matters a great deal.' And she wept with her son.

Advent is the season to weep. It's the time to admit the brutal facts – to be honest about the way the world is, and the way that we are, and to admit that everything is not okay. Something is seriously wrong. So often we seek to numb ourselves from reality, to paper over what is wrong. We pretend that it's not really there or that it won't be as bad as we fear if we only remain 'positive'. Advent isn't about negativity, but it is about truth-telling. It's about waiting in the barefaced reality of what we confess is truly present.

Advent is also a season to remind us of our utter dependence on God – that only he has the power to change things. Advent is therefore a season of longing that God would come and do what only God can do. Ultimately, it is about hope – the hope of change, transformation and the restoration of things to the way they were always meant to be. Yet this hope only comes through a liminal season of waiting.

We all find waiting so hard, which is why Christmas will always remain more popular than Advent. Yet we lose so much if we only have the immediacy of Christmas preparations in our minds as we journey through Advent. In Advent, we join Elizabeth, Zechariah, Mary, Simeon and Anna in their waiting for the first coming of Jesus Christ, to rescue and redeem Israel. And our horizons are even broader as we await his second coming, to make all things new.

We find a vision of God's ultimate future for the world at the end of the book of Revelation, with its stunning depiction of creation restored and renewed. God will make his dwelling with us, wiping away every tear from our eyes, and bringing an end to death and mourning and crying and pain. Our hearts long for this restored reality – this is what we were created for! It is the day that the Old Testament prophets looked forward to, when swords are beaten into ploughshares and spears into pruning hooks, as war is replaced by fruitful production (Isaiah 2:4) – the day when the wolf lives with the lamb and the leopard lies down with the kid in cosmic peace and harmony (Isaiah 11:6). All are invited to 'come' – all who are thirsty and who wish for the free gift of the water of life (Revelation 22:17) – as our longing for God echoes his for us.

In the meantime, we cry, 'Oh, that you would rend the heavens and come down', with the prophet Isaiah (64:1). This is the Advent yearning of our hearts as well. Come, make things right again! Come, do what we cannot do ourselves! How we need Advent to sharpen our focus on this ultimate reality. As Chaplain Mike writes:

> *We have turned Advent into something else.* We've made it simply about preparing for Christmas. That certainly is part of it, but it's not the whole message of this season. Traditionally, Advent has been a *penitential* season, like Lent. It's a time for self-examination. It's a time for confession of sins. It's a time to humble ourselves and be honest with ourselves and recognise that, in many ways, we're a mess and our families are a mess, and our churches are a mess, and the nations are a mess, and our world is a mess.
>
> *Advent is a time to recognise that unless God saves us we will not be saved.*[16]

Sacred practice – prayer

Simone Weil, a Jewish writer, says that 'waiting patiently in expectation is the foundation of the spiritual life'. Eugene Peterson writes that 'waiting in prayer is a disciplined refusal to act before God acts'. He expounds:

Another will is greater, wiser and more intelligent than my own. So I wait. Waiting means that there is Another whom I trust and from whom I receive. My will, important and essential as it is, finds a Will that is more important, more essential... In prayer we are aware that God is in action and that when the circumstances are ready, when others are in the right place and when my heart is prepared, I will be called into action. Waiting in prayer is a disciplined refusal to act before God acts. Waiting is our participation in the process that results in the 'time fulfilled'.[17]

In this sense, and consistent with Acts 1, the first assignment of the church is to do nothing.

In recent years, the archbishops of Canterbury and York have sought to call the church back to the ancient practice of 'novena' – the nine-day period of prayer that traditionally falls between the Feast of Ascension (when Jesus physically departed earth for heaven) and the Feast of Pentecost (when the first disciples were gifted with the presence of the Holy Spirit). It marks a time when Jesus' disciples are said to have prayed constantly – stuck as they were in an in-between place, waiting to see what God would do next.

These disciples, following Easter Sunday, had already spent 40 days with the risen Christ, as he proved to them the reality of his risen life and spoke to them about the kingdom of God. There was much that had not been revealed to them about what was to come; nonetheless, before Jesus ascended into heaven, they received both a promise and an instruction. The promise was of the coming of the Holy Spirit, who would baptise them in a matter of days in a manner akin to how John had baptised. This coming of the Holy Spirit would give them power to be Jesus' witnesses to the ends of the earth. The instruction was to stay in Jerusalem and to wait for the promise of the Father. As a result, the disciples, together with some women and the family of Jesus, were constantly devoting themselves to prayer in those days between Ascension and Pentecost – caught in the space between.

Because of the familiarity of the story of Pentecost, we can too easily lose the narrative tension of those nine in-between days following Jesus' ascension into heaven. The disciples could not have known *exactly* what it was for which they were waiting. What was this new power that they would receive? What might baptism in the Holy Spirit even mean? How would the Spirit come upon them? The disciples would, of course, have read about manifestations of the Spirit in the Old Testament – on craftsmen and kings, strong men and prophets. They had seen the Spirit at work in the life of Jesus, and they knew of the promise for the Spirit to be poured out on all people. But none of this is to say they had any *definitive* idea of what Jesus' promise would look like in reality. In spite of this, and in the void, they waited.

The disciples' waiting was not empty, because it was contingent on the promise that had been given to them by Jesus. It was not passive, because they were leaning into this promise, not sitting back and twiddling their thumbs. It was not about their own wants and wishes, but an openness to all that God was seeking to give them, trusting that their heavenly Father delights to give good gifts to his children – or as Luke phrases it, to give the Holy Spirit to those who ask.

We might say one more thing about the waiting of the disciples between Ascension and Pentecost – it was obedient. They did what they were asked to do. In contrast, Michael Green argues, 'It would probably not be an exaggeration to say that disobedience is one of the main characteristics of modern Christianity. We know what Jesus teaches but we do not do it.'[18]

The temptation in waiting is always for us to take things into our own hands, to engineer the outcome that we are looking for, because we are perennially controlled by the fear of missing out (FOMO). FOMO was conceptualised with the rise of social media and the perceived need to remain connected, in spite of the adverse effects on well-being that this has.[19] It also describes a range of other anxieties regarding absence from social engagement – such as not being on the inside of a conversation, not having watched the latest show on Netflix, or not

attending a wedding or party. Through a process of 'relative deprivation', FOMO leads to an impression of our having less, which makes
us feel dissatisfied with our experiences. It is particularly exploited by
modern advertising, which preys on our desire to have everything that
we see others around us having.

When God asks us to wait, this is a difficult task within a modern culture underwritten by the social anxiety of FOMO. There is so much in
life to have and to experience, so the narrative goes, yet so little time in
which to do this. The pace of life gets only faster, and we are exposed
to ever-widening horizons, such that even the smallest amount of
waiting can feel like an almighty waste in our endless drive to use our
time as 'productively' as possible. However, in this we miss something
of paramount importance. Who we become in our waiting is just as
important as that for which we are waiting. Besides, as Louie Giglio,
founder of the Passion Movement, has said, if we're truly waiting on
God – the God of endless abundance and eternal provision – then we
won't miss out on anything.

By ourselves, we can struggle with impatience and be overcome by the
agony of divine delay. For this reason, Jesus teaches twice in parables
in Luke's gospel about the need to persist in prayer.

In Luke 11, Jesus asks his disciples to imagine that they are entertain-
ing a friend at short notice and are short of bread. They head to a
neighbour at night to ask for provision, and the neighbour turns them
down point-blank. (Jesus is being humorous here as in the Middle
East, with its embedded culture of hospitality, this would simply not
occur – just as God does not turn down point-blank our own requests
to him for the things that we need.) In spite of this, says Jesus, it will
be your 'shameless audacity' (v. 8) in persisting with your request
that will lead your neighbour to get up and give you what you ask.
The point is, how much more will God respond to our 'shameless
audacity' in prayer for him to give us all that we need. So, Jesus
says, 'Ask and it will be given to you; seek and you will find; knock
and the door will be opened to you. For everyone who asks receives;

the one who seeks finds; and to the one who knocks, the door will be opened' (vv. 9–10).

In Luke 18, Jesus tells his disciples a further parable explicitly 'to show them that they should always pray and not give up' (v. 1). Imagine again, Jesus says, a judge who cares neither for people nor God – once more, the situation is farcical and humorous. There was once a widow who sought justice against an adversary and who kept being turned down by the judge. Eventually the judge, simply for the sake of his own peace and quiet, gave in to her demands so that she wouldn't persist in 'bothering' him. The point is, how much more will God, who cares so deeply for us, be willing to act when we pray and don't give up? 'And will not God bring about justice for his chosen ones, who cry out to him day and night? Will he keep putting them off? I tell you, he will see that they get justice, and quickly' (vv. 7–8). The thing in question, according to this parable, is not God's willingness to act, but the persistence of our faith expressed through prayer.

Yet still, God's notion of time seems so very out of sync with our own. Scripture tells us that the heroes of the Bible sometimes had to wait not just days, weeks or months, but years, even decades. In such painfully elongated seasons of waiting, we can only fall back on postures of trust and hope – trust in the God who is good and loving, powerful and able, and hope that this God has a future for us with plans that are immeasurably more than we could ever ask or imagine, but which may look nothing like what we had conceived. We express our trust in God, and we put our hope in him, through prayer. The practice of prayer assures us in faith that if we're waiting on God, then we won't miss out on anything.

I was impressed with the faith of my youngest child during the first coronavirus lockdown. She had been enjoying the YouTube channel '5-minute crafts', and wanted to make some crystals. When we looked together at what this involved, the final step was to wait 20 days for something significant to happen. My wife Sarah and I were both unconvinced by this, suggesting she try something that brought about more instantaneous results. We were, rightly, put in our place. 'No,' our daughter told us. 'I want to do this. I'll wait 20 days. It will be worth it.'

Sacred stories

Historical saint – Nelson Mandela

'Until I changed myself, I could not change others,' said Nelson Mandela, expressing a deeply Christian idea. For Mandela, it was in the space between – in the time of waiting – that he was transformed. For all of us, there comes a time in the liminal seasons of life when we can so easily be taken captive by bitterness. Perhaps the most striking thing about Mandela was that when on 27 February 1990 he emerged from 27 years of waiting in prison, he was a man at peace. He had waited patiently for the promise of racial reconciliation. The title of his famous autobiography reminds us of what really goes on in the space between – 'the long walk to freedom'.

The faith of Nelson Mandela is not uncomplicated, and it was not always something that he spoke about publicly. Mandela was raised and schooled as a Methodist, an experience he was always fond of. Yet he was concerned about speaking publicly of his own faith for fear of creating division or, worse still, of using religion as a political tool, as did the apartheid regime. The Dutch Reformed Church had furnished apartheid with its religious underpinnings by suggesting that Afrikaners were God's chosen people and that blacks were a subservient species. In the mindset of Afrikaners, apartheid and the church went hand-in-hand. So Mandela had to be cautious – but this did not mean that faith was not at the centre of his being.

Mandela did not wish to resort to the use of violence until all other routes had failed. This phase of his activism may feel impossible to justify; however, it has been argued that Mandela's Christian faith influenced his strategy even during the more militant portion of his protest against the government. The targets Mandela chose, and the way in which the group timed its attacks, were a clear message that he intended to target the government, not the civilians it claimed to serve. In 1962, Mandela was sentenced to life in prison for his role in organising bombings of police stations. Ultimately, Mandela's Christian faith would lead him from violent action to peaceful reconciliation.

While in prison, Mandela lost faith in revolution and in communism. His prison cell on Robben Island had something of a monastic spirit about it, filled as it was with books and manuscripts. Christ was not the only prophet who served as an inspiration to Mandela in his cell. Mahatma Gandhi's practice of non-violence, inspired as it was by Christ's sermon on the mount, came to be seen by Mandela as more effective than violent confrontation when applied within a society that shares the same Christian and humanist values.

In prison, Mandela was a man of discipline. This enabled him to study law as a University of London external student and helped him to learn Afrikaans, the language of most of the white minority. Most centrally, it aided him to overcome his personal bitterness at the estrangement from his wife, children and community during his imprisonment. Mandela was always able to keep in mind the bigger picture of who he was and what he was about. When he was asked about prosecuting whites from the apartheid regime, he replied, 'Prosecution? I'm not interested in prosecution. I'm interested in building a nation.' At the moment of his release, Mandela again stressed the importance of internal renewal ahead of external change. He wrote: 'As I walked out the door toward the gate that would lead to my freedom, I knew if I didn't leave my bitterness and hatred behind, I'd still be in prison.' As he also said: 'Resentment is like drinking poison and then hoping it will kill your enemies.'

The Commission for Truth and Reconciliation, founded by President Mandela and led by Bishop Desmond Tutu, is perhaps the most concrete example we have of Mandela's Christian faith. Instead of the vengeance and reprisals that had been expected and feared after years of interracial violence, the commission focused on confession and forgiveness. Most who admitted misdeeds and even crimes – whether committed in the name of, or in opposition to, apartheid – received amnesty. Many returned to civil life, exonerated by their admission of guilt. It could be said that what Gandhi was to non-violent resistance, Mandela was to reconciliation with an oppressor.

It is Mandela's actions which chiefly speak of the power of his faith. However, his words do as well, as upon his liberation Mandela took opportunities to speak at substantial Christian events. Two of these were the Zionist Christian Church's Easter conferences, once in 1992 and again in 1994. In the latter of these conferences he shared the following:

> The Good News borne by our risen Messiah, who chose not one race, who chose not one country, who chose not one language, who chose not one tribe, who chose all of humankind! Our Messiah, who came to us in the form of a mortal man, but who by his suffering and crucifixion attained immortality. Our Messiah, born like an outcast in a stable, and executed like a criminal on the cross.[20]

Mandela's moral stature as a leader has inevitably invoked messianic imagery, both during his life and even more so after his death. The BBC presenter Evan Davis told listeners that Mandela should be ranked alongside Jesus in 'the pantheon of virtue' and the political editor of *The Telegraph*, Peter Oborne, wrote: 'There are very few human beings who can be compared to Jesus Christ. Nelson Mandela is one.' In contrast, Mandela never had an overly romantic view of who he was. He once said of himself: 'I'm not a saint, unless you think of a saint as a sinner who keeps on trying.' His story reminds us of the precious formation of character that can take place in times of waiting.

At the end of his life, his long-time friend Bishop Malusi Mpumlwana said Mandela's favourite blessing as he died:

May the Lord bless you and keep you.
May the Lord make his face to shine upon you and be gracious
   to you.
May the Lord look upon you with kindness, and give you peace.

Contemporary saint

This is the story, in their own words, of a friend who has journeyed, or is still journeying, through the space between.

Waiting in a place of brokenness. My waiting hasn't been a straightforward waiting for one particular thing. It has been waiting for healing, waiting for direction, waiting for justice. It has had twists and turns and what has felt like a script that the writer of a TV soap couldn't come up with.

My default setting is to ignore the pain just to enable me to cope. I don't like sitting in the pain or to have to wait. I would prefer to be mended now and to get on with life. There was disappointment with God. Could another disaster really happen? Why did he seemingly answer my prayers for other people but not for me and my family? There was confusion and fear in the waiting when the direction I thought I was taking with God, to lift myself out of failure, was changed and plunged into another trauma. There was frustration as I felt too broken to be useful. I couldn't see a way forward and in fact needed time to process what was happening before I could do anything. I was not able to look forward to the future; my ability to hope had gone. I feared hope because the next thing might be taken from me too. I have written this in the past tense – 'There was…' To some extent there still is disappointment, confusion, fear and frustration. It is sometimes still hard to hope, especially for specifics; however, God has brought me on a journey in which he has held and taught me through the pain. I am still waiting, but I am also learning more ways to wait with God.

At first all I could do was to cling on to God. It wasn't easy to pray, and my experiences clouded the way I read the Bible. The solid ground that

I had stood on before was now wobbly, and I was unsure of everything. I imagined that I was holding on to a round boulder with my little finger and could slip off at any point. A friend had a picture from God of me lying on a huge rock, like a sandstone pavement. My perspective began to change. I couldn't fall off this huge Rock – I didn't even need to hold on, and I could just lie there. And so I did, until I was ready to try to make some steps forward. I often come back to sit or lie on this Rock. Later it was suggested to me that despite feeling broken, perhaps it was time to throw myself into something. This came at the right time and so I was able to. By getting involved my perspective began to broaden, I could focus on more positive things and enjoy myself again.

However, everywhere I went I still carried with me the weight of my experiences and pain. It felt like I was two people, hiding what was going on inside and dealing with it alone – though I wasn't dealing with it, as I didn't know how to. I needed to learn to accept what had happened and to honestly bring it to God.

Two other friends spoke to me about lamenting. This rarely taught form of prayer has been so helpful. Crying out to God about my experiences, shouting, praying through all the emotions that I was carrying inside. The simple question 'How long, O Lord?' repeated in prayer, the words sometimes came out in tongues or groans from deep within. The Holy Spirit helping me to voice what I couldn't.

Another form of prayer that God has taught me is to pray using his name (Proverbs 18:10; Psalm 20:1–2). When I need guiding, I imagine Jesus as a good shepherd leading me; when I need comfort, I pray to the comforter; if I need protection, then I ask my heavenly Father. This lifts me, redirecting my thoughts from myself to God, who is far greater and gives me a more secure perspective in the waiting.

God has taught me ways to connect honestly with him in prayer. He has given me glimpses of hope through Bible passages and the prayers of faithful people. The waiting goes on, but as I remind myself of these things, I find a way to continue a day at a time, enjoying God's goodness surrounding me.

A prayer for when you're stuck in the waiting place

Father, can I be honest?
I am tired of waiting.
Waiting is hard, painful, exhausting.
But I know that learning to wait well is a beautiful, sanctifying,
*   hope-giving thing.*
So help me wait well.
Help me cling to you as I wait.
Please, Lord, let your peace rule in my heart.
Help me live by your grace each day of this waiting.
And help me bring you glory as I wait expectantly.
In Jesus' name, Amen.
Marlo Schalesky[21]

Questions for reflection

1 How would you reflect on your ability to wait for something?
2 What place do the lament psalms – and lamentation or complaint in general – have within your practice of prayer?
3 What is there from this chapter that gives you the greatest encouragement to wait?

4

The place of exile: when life feels alien

How can we sing the songs of the Lord while in a foreign land?
PSALM 137:4

Seeking to forget makes exile all the longer; the secret of redemption lies in remembrance.[1]

Human emotions – alienation and lostness

The experience of exile is one of being in a 'foreign land' – whether this be an alien place, a peculiar circumstance or an unusual season. It can bring an overwhelming sense of being lost. This carries powerful feelings of not belonging, of somehow not fitting in. Within the framework of our basic needs as explained by Abraham Maslow, our physiological needs (food, water, warmth, rest) might be met, but there could be significant gaps around our needs above this – perhaps feeling less safe and secure than we once did, or lacking a sense of intimate community.

As much as our culture increasingly understands identity as something that is self-generated – 'be who you are' or 'be who you want to be' – we are inescapably formed through the ties that bind us to things beyond ourselves. There are two of these in particular.

First, we are tied to *place* – to land with its complexities of geography and history. We feel a sense of home in relation to our knowledge of space. There are settings that are familiar to us and areas we know our way around – both the official routes and those off the beaten track. We have deep memories engrained in a place. However, we should not be surprised that we feel such a tie to land and to earth – after all, in the second Genesis account of the creation of human beings, the man, *adam*, is formed from the dust of the ground, *adamah*. That the two should be so closely connected is a thing of mystery, yet it is an intricate part of the way in which we have been made.

When we are 'at home', we know the landmarks; they give us points of reference. We recognise something around us, a feature of the land, and it helps us to locate our position. This gives us confidence that we know where we are so that we can take the next step on our journey. Margaret Silf usefully explains the difference between 'maps and guidebooks' and 'landmarks'.[2] Silf notes that a map or guidebook can be read in an armchair, telling us, 'Go this way, or else!' or, 'Fifty ways to climb the ladder of perfection.' She observes how 'they all teach you how to swim without getting wet'. She contrasts this with landmarks which refuse to let you do this and which are no use until, and unless, you're on the road:

> They are effective only in that they *connect* where you are, in your own life experience, to a point of recognition and orientation, for your own story and for the whole human story.

However, the pain of exile is this: there are no landmarks. The ones that used to guide us are gone. We look out and all that we see feels unfamiliar – it has no meaning for us and cannot help to orient us on our journey. All landmarks are about local knowledge and must be experienced first-hand, yet in exile we can only live off second-hand experience. We have no history with the location we're in; it carries no memory for us. Such is the experience of exile, and it can be an incredibly difficult place in which to live. At times like this, inescapably it seems, we can lack confidence and lose heart.

When we moved to Preston in 2016, it took time, for example, to work out where it was best to park on a trip into town; where we'd most enjoy walking our dog, Alfie; what the quickest route was on to the Guild Wheel (a 21-mile circular route around the city) from where we lived; and which lanes we needed to go down to get to the canal and a local park most easily. This was all about local knowledge, of appreciating a place in specifics, not just generalities. There was a lot of trial and error, and plenty of getting lost and finding our way again. It takes time to really know a place.

Second, we are tied to *people*. This usually means one's immediate family and relations – the household in which we were brought up. This is where we learn so much about who we are, how we behave, how to deal with conflict and how to express love. However, more widely we feel tied to those who are 'like us'. We are connected to people who share a common outlook on the world, who have values like ours and who express themselves in similar customs and habits. We speak of 'kindred spirits' – those who at an intuitive level see things the same way that we do, which brings a synergy in journeying the road of life together. For this reason, Eugene Peterson describes exile bluntly as 'being where we don't want to be with people we don't want to be with'.[3]

Exile most obviously arises when we move location and lose a sense of home. However, an exilic experience might equally emerge from circumstances that suddenly make us feel that we're in a world to which we no longer belong: an illness, afflicting either ourselves or someone we love; a change of job; a falling into debt. There are so many possibilities, yet they each share a sense of radical change, a feeling of lostness, an uncertainty as to the way forward and a loss of confidence as to who we are. Exile can happen instantaneously or it can take place almost without noticing. Either way, a dislocation is perceived that creates a distance between ourselves and what is known or comfortable. We lose that sense of being 'at home' and feel that the things around us are not the way they should really be.

Sacred scriptures

Old Testament – Abram and Israel

Abram in exile (Genesis 12)

Genesis 12 is a significant marker in the book of Genesis, and indeed in the whole of salvation history. Yet there are crucial aspects of the story of the call of Abram that I have frequently overlooked, and it has only been in some of the changes of location that we have made as a family that I have felt a deeper respect for Abram and understood more fully the cost of God's call upon his life.

> The Lord had said to Abram, 'Go from your country, your people and your father's household to the land I will show you.'
> GENESIS 12:1

What a challenging call this was! Land, people, household: these are the very ties that bind in the ancient Near East. In the world in which Abram lived, it would be impossible to imagine life apart from them; hence, when God calls Abram to 'up sticks' and walk away from these things, we are speaking of a radical instruction. Without a tie to land and to place, there is a sense of dislocation; without a tie to kindred, there is a sense of disconnection; without a tie to family, there is a loss of belonging. These are the very things that we humanly rely upon to live safely and comfortably in the world, yet they are the substance of what Abram is asked to surrender. His network of meaningful, life-giving connections is severed. As for replacements, Abram must go to a land that God will show him, but which has not yet been revealed; he is promised a family that will become a great nation, of which there is no sign in the present.

In short, Abram had to renounce all the certainties of the past, to face all the uncertainties of the future and in the meantime to live in the difficult space between. All of this makes me marvel at his radical obedience. One of Abram's brothers, Haran, died young. His other brother, Nahor, and his wife, Milkah, never even set out on the journey of obedience, preferring instead to stay at home. Abram's father, Terah, headed for the promised land but settled part-way in Harran and died there. Only Abram, together with his wife Sarai, his nephew Lot and those whom they had acquired in Harran, journeyed all the way to the promised land. Abram chose to embrace exile with his dependence cast upon the God who had called him and who had spoken promises to him. The space between can only be sustained by the presence of God and the promises of God.

Israel in exile

Abram's pilgrimage into exile came before the nation of Israel had even come into being. It was a choice made out of obedience to God. However, when Israel encountered their own exile in the sixth century BC, it was precisely because of their disobedience. The northern kingdom had already been defeated by the Assyrians in the eighth century BC. The captivity of the southern kingdom in Babylon is presented in scripture as a punishment for Judah's idolatry and her refusal to follow the ways of God. Perhaps the primary passage on the subject is Deuteronomy 29:24–28:

> All the nations will ask: 'Why has the Lord done this to this land?…' And the answer will be: 'It is because this people abandoned the covenant of the Lord… They went off and worshipped other gods… Therefore the Lord's anger burned… In furious anger and in great wrath the Lord uprooted them from their land and thrust them into another land, as it is now.'

Nebuchadnezzar began a siege of Jerusalem in December 589BC, during which the city endured terrible deprivation. Eventually, Nebuchadnezzar broke through Jerusalem's walls. King Zedekiah and his followers attempted to escape but were captured on the plains of Jericho and taken to Riblah. After seeing his sons killed, Zedekiah was blinded, bound and taken captive to Babylon, where he remained a prisoner until his death. The fall of Jerusalem saw the city plundered and razed to the ground and, most horrifying of all, Solomon's temple destroyed. Most of the elite were taken into captivity in Babylon, while a small number of people were left behind in order to tend the land.

In exile, all the landmarks that gave the nation its orientation and identity were gone – covenant, king, land and temple. This left many questions in its wake. Surely this was the end of the unique relationship that God had had with the Jews? Who would they follow now that the king was rendered powerless? How could they even worship God given that the temple was destroyed? Who were they as a people, given their ejection from the land? This was a national shaming and a horrifying experience of judgement from God. It was a shocking time of dislocation, isolation and loss. 'How can we sing the songs of the Lord while in a foreign land?' (Psalm 137:4) was the refrain.

Although the people of God suffered greatly and faced powerful cultural pressures in a foreign land, astoundingly, in the mercy of God, the experience of exile turned out to have many positives. It forced Israel to re-engage with their founding stories, as they asked deep questions of who they were. Any experience of exile forces an engagement with notions of identity, and Israel had to look back in their story to who God had called them to be. The creation story is but one powerful example of this. The Babylonians told a story in which the creation of the world was a product of the violence of the gods as Marduk defeated Tiamat, ripping open her womb and spreading it out to form the fabric of the cosmos. In this, human beings were merely the playthings of the gods. The Jews instead told an altogether more beautiful story of a God who brings order from chaos by the power of his word – forming spaces for creation and then filling them with life. Human beings are his image and his likeness in the world, the representation to creation of the divine nature. Without the experience of exile, such reflections might not have been so sharply formed.

Within this process, the Jewish people studied the law – the Torah – and wrote down much of the Old Testament in its present form. With the fall of the temple and the loss of corrupt kings and false prophets, there was a new repentance and a fresh returning to God and his ways. There was a renewed hope as prophets promised that God would restore David's fallen dynasty (Hosea 3:5; Amos 9:11) and give Judah a 'new covenant' to replace the one that they had broken (Jeremiah 31:31–34). Elders supervised the Jewish communities, and Ezekiel was one of several prophets who kept alive the hope of one day returning home. This was also likely the period when synagogues were first established, as the Jewish people observed the sabbath and religious holidays, practised circumcision and substituted prayers for former ritual sacrifices in the temple.

In all of this, there was the surprising encouragement from God through the prophet Jeremiah to 'make home' in exile. The words '"For I know the plans I have for you," declares the Lord, "plans to prosper you and not to harm you, plans to give you hope and a future"' (Jeremiah 29:11) are amongst the best loved in the Bible today. However, their context is seldom appreciated. Jeremiah is writing to the exiles of Judah in Babylon with good news that God promises to bring them back to the promised land. Yet this will not happen as soon as they might have hoped – not until 70 years are over (v. 15). In the meantime, they should do what must have been unthinkable for them:

> Build houses and settle down; plant gardens and eat what they produce. Marry and have sons and daughters; find wives for your sons and give your daughters in marriage, so that they too may have sons and daughters. Increase in number there; do not decrease. Also, seek the peace and prosperity of the city to which I have carried you into exile. Pray to the Lord for it, because if it prospers, you too will prosper.
> JEREMIAH 29:5–7

Sometimes, God asks the unimaginable – 'make home in exile' – of us too; I know I've experienced this. Don't just dream of an idealised place or future where everything will be okay again (it probably won't) and sit there waiting for it to drop into our laps. Find God's peace – his wholeness, well-being, flourishing – in exactly the places and seasons in which we are currently located. As the saying goes, 'If the grass looks greener on the other side, start watering the grass you're standing on.' One of the perils of the space between is that we become too introspective. Instead, God through Jeremiah focuses Judah's attention outwards. Looking out for the needs of others in a new way – through prayer and service – is always a life-giving posture for our own seasons of exile.

In time, Cyrus the Great became king of Persia and the Jewish exiles were allowed to return to the promised land. The trickle back was fairly slow – it seems to have taken at least a century – and it was not a return to the same. There was certainly a hope and a future where once there had been nothing at all. The walls were rebuilt and even a new temple constructed, more modestly at first under the governor Zerubbabel, and then more magnificently during the reign of Herod the Great when it was completely refurbished and the original structure totally overhauled. Nonetheless, a sense persisted that, even at the end of the second temple period, God's people remained in exile. The original prophecy of 70 years in exile (Jeremiah 25:8–14; 29:10–14) was reinterpreted as 70 weeks of years, or 490 years (Daniel 9:24). The wait for the end of exile continued.

Psalm 137

Psalm 137 is one of the few psalms that gives us a sense of its historical context. It is clearly a psalm of lament set during Israel's time in exile in Babylon. There is a persistent theme throughout the psalm of remembering and not forgetting. Verse 1 speaks of remembering Zion, or Jerusalem; verses 5–6 contemplate the horror of forgetting Jerusalem and of not remembering; finally, there is a petition for God to remember the Edomites, Israel's brother nation, for their complicity in the fall of Jerusalem. This speaks powerfully into the reality that the space between, as a place of exile, is a place of needing to know deeply one's identity. The irony for Israel was that they had forgotten who they were in their homeland, failing to honour God and being distracted by idols around them, such that it took exile for them to remember who they really were.

Psalm 137 is set in three sections, of three verses each.

Verses 1–3 speak of the grief, shame and oppression of exile. Living in Jerusalem had been a sign that Israel were God's chosen people. The belief had been that they were always impregnable because of God's protection. Exile shook the foundation of Israel's faith, just as times of disruption do for us. Now, by the rivers of Babylon, there is weeping as what has been lost is remembered. The psalm is a reminder that our faith is not merely spiritual, and that physical landmarks and places are deeply significant, carrying meaning and memory for us. In exile, harps are hung up, as the present does not feel like a time for singing. For myself, though I love to worship God in song, I have always found the space between to be a difficult place in which to sing. The notes and syllables do not resound in the way that they used to. In this psalm, the pain is made worse by the taunting and mockery of Israel's oppressors who are demanding a song as a further exercise in humiliation.

In spite of the pain of exile (vv. 1–3) and the difficulty of singing in such a context (v. 4), there is a resolve that memory will not be lost (vv. 5–6). This is 'nostalgia' (derived from the ancient Greek *nostos*, 'homecoming', and *algos*, 'pain' – encapsulating the emotion's bittersweet pull), which research shows makes us feel less lonely and more optimistic about the future; more connected to our past selves and, by extension, to our future selves. Memory here gives meaning. The memory of Jerusalem is harnessed to look forward in hope and to centre Israel on who they really are. As Sotirios Christou has said, 'In the hopelessness of being in exile, holding on to Jerusalem in the imagination of their faith and in their hearts is the harbinger of hope.'[4] Brueggemann agrees: 'This is a song for the long haul, for those not able to see the change, but knowing that hope for change can be sustained for the long term. The psalm does not despair. Hope is resilient here.'[5]

This is akin to the experience of Viktor Frankl in Auschwitz. A prominent Viennese psychiatrist before the war, Frankl was well placed to observe the way that both he and others coped, or didn't cope, through the experience of the Holocaust. He found that everything can be taken away from people *except* the ability to derive meaning in any given set of circumstances. This means that those who were able to sustain their moral and spiritual selves could turn even the most horrific outer experiences into an inner triumph. What Jim Collins terms 'the Stockdale Paradox'[6] accords with this: the notion of confronting the most brutal facts of your current reality (the externals) while retaining faith that you will prevail in the end (the internals), regardless of current circumstances. In Psalm 137, such faith is anchored by the memory of home which provides hope for the future. For followers of Jesus Christ, his resurrection – which we celebrate in prayer, worship and Holy Communion – means that we are always carried by hope.

This reality of confronting the brutal facts comes to the fore in verses 7–9. Here the facts are not just the externals of what has happened, but the internals of the emotions it has provoked. We might feel embarrassed that such sentiments are not fully redeemed – 'Happy is the one who seizes your infants and dashes them against the rocks' – however, there is a principle at work here that we should not miss for our own navigation of the space between. There is no suggestion that Israel followed through with such actions, barbaric as they would have been. Nonetheless, there is something vital about vocalising even the darkest sentiments in our soul, in order to bring them to the light and to hand them to God. Far more healthy this than to express romantic sentiments to God in our words while allowing our souls to fester with unresolved hatred and resentment. Such darkness is here expressed to God because it is for him to act – vengeance belongs to the Lord (Deuteronomy 32:35; Romans 12:17–19).

Jesus Christ – incarnation

Jesus Christ knows what it is to live in exile, because of the incarnation. Philippians 2:7 speaks of Jesus emptying himself, taking the form of a slave, being born in human likeness. In patristic theology, the term 'kenosis' (drawing on the Greek word for 'emptying') was employed to describe the action of the Father and the Son in the incarnation. Marie-Jose Baudinet has expressed the incarnation in this way:

> In short, kenosis is, in the context of the great economist's expenditure, the sacrifice of the Father who exiles His Son from His glory during His earthly life. This does not mean that the Son ceases to participate in the Father's glory, but, rather, that He renounces making it visible.[7]

In the same vein, Karl Barth, in his celebrated *Church Dogmatics* (Vol. IV, 1 and 2), characterises the Father's sending of the Son into the world with the words, 'The Way of the Son Into the Far Country', as he describes Jesus following the path of the prodigal son from the famous parable in Luke's gospel. Just as the prodigal son travelled to 'a distant country' (Luke 15:13), heading into the depths of debauchery and sin, so Jesus, the Son, makes the same journey, taking the chaos and calamity of the prodigal son upon himself. This crossing over into the far country is radical, risky and extravagant. Decisively, the Son of God carries out this journey not in disobedience but in perfect obedience to his Father.

Care does need to be exercised in understanding the incarnation as a type of exile. We do not say that Jesus' incarnation was exilic in the sense that it indicated the paucity of a physical earth as against the glory of a spiritual heaven – for all that God created is good and one day he will renew all things to make a new heaven and a new earth. Rather, exile is a suitable metaphor for Christ's coming into our *fallen* world. John 1 affirms both the goodness of creation and the sense of alienation of Christ within this disordered world. Verses 3–4 tell us: 'Through him all things were made; without him nothing was made that has been made. In him was life, and that life was the light of all mankind.' Yet verses 10–11 go on to say: 'He was in the world, and though the world was made through him, the world did not recognise him. He came to that which was his own, but his own did not receive him.'

Isaiah 53:3 (NRSV) expresses a similar idea:

> He was despised and rejected by others; a man of suffering and
> acquainted with infirmity; as one from whom others hide their
> faces he was despised, and we held him of no account.

Jesus himself articulated this sense of exile as a way of understanding
his existence on the earth. One day someone came to Jesus, promising boldly that they would follow Jesus wherever he went – the sense
was that to follow Jesus was to go 'from victory to victory'. However,
Jesus reframed the path of discipleship as being more akin to living
in exile. He said, 'Foxes have dens and birds have nests, but the Son
of Man has nowhere to lay his head' (Luke 9:58). Jesus was nomadic, a
wanderer, a pilgrim during his days on the earth. He did not find home,
but instead was acquainted with exile, hostility and loneliness. There
was something deeply restless about his earthly pilgrimage.

Jesus also knew of exile in a specific way from his earliest days. Mary
and Joseph were forced to flee to Egypt with Jesus when he was
only a toddler. The despotic Herod the Great, together with the Jerusalem establishment, had been disturbed by the news the Magi had
brought of one born to be the king of the Jews. As soon as the angel
appeared to Joseph in a dream, they travelled in the night – that
liminal time we saw in the Jacob story – to stay in Egypt until the
death of Herod. My own church in Preston, together with so many
others, has become home to a number of asylum seekers who have
sought refuge in our land from a host of violent regimes and tragic
circumstances. What comfort to savour that Jesus is well acquainted
with such journeys into exile; that he was an asylum seeker long
before they were.

Exile at its most painful extent would be known by Christ in his cry of
dereliction on the cross: 'Why have you forsaken me?' (Matthew 27:46).
In his death, Jesus was 'exiled' from the land of the living. Through
all of this, he lived out Israel's story of exile in its fullness, in order to
finally bring it to an end. His rising from the grave and ascension to the

Father are a homecoming in which all are invited to leave their own experiences of exile far behind.

New Testament – John at Patmos

My favourite book of the Bible has always been the book of Revelation.[8] When we read that John was on Patmos 'because of the word of God and the testimony of Jesus' (Revelation 1:9), it is often inferred that he had been exiled as punishment for his faith. While we have no definitive proof that Patmos was used as a penal colony, nor even that it was inhabited at the time of John's writing, this makes no difference to our use of the book here. Whether John was forced on to Patmos or chose to go there, something about that experience opened up fresh horizons for him. John notes that he is our 'brother and companion in the suffering and kingdom and patient endurance that are ours in Jesus' (Revelation 1:9). The 'suffering' refers to the pain of the present moment; 'kingdom' to our future hope; and 'patient endurance' as what is needed to live well in the space between.

John's challenge concerns where we make our home. For the churches of Asia Minor to whom he wrote, significant temptation would have come from the communication of powerful myths regarding the Roman Empire – of peace, victory, faith and eternity[9] – as well as from local expressions of empire through the social, economic, political and religious structures of everyday life. It is clear from the royal pronouncements in Revelation 2 and 3 that churches were mixed in their resistance to these claims and lures – some stood firm, living as exiles in anticipation of the coming of another kingdom, or empire, while others were more accommodating, making a home in a culture that should have remained alien to them. John writes, therefore, both to comfort the afflicted and to afflict the comfortable. Scenes in the book of Revelation alternate between the reassuring and the provocative.

Even numbers are marshalled by John to make theological points in ways that would have been familiar to his first audience, but can often miss us today.[10] The things of God come as square numbers, in particular the 144 (12x12) thousand of his people in chapter 7 and the New Jerusalem in chapter 21. The enemies of God come in triangular numbers, not least the number of the beast in chapter 13. But the life we live for God in the present is marked by rectangular numbers, such as the 42 months or 1,260 days mentioned several times between chapters 11 and 13. Rectangles look a bit like squares, but they are also composed of two triangles. This is to say, they share the characteristics of both. In other words, we are citizens of both worlds – the heavenly and the earthly – and find ourselves caught in the space between. The kingdom of God has come in the person of Jesus, yet we continue to live in a fallen world ahead of the day when all things are made new. This is why 'patient endurance' is required to inhabit the disruptive and liminal overlap of the 'suffering' and the 'kingdom' of Revelation 1:9.

The book of Revelation gives a powerful cosmic 'unveiling' of the reality of earth seen from heaven's perspective, and the reality of the present seen from the perspective of eternity. We are given a behind-the-scenes view of the world, as well as being transported into its ultimate future so that we can glimpse God's purposes for the present. The effect is to blow open the imagination of the reader to transcendent reality. Our mindsets can easily shrink down, so what John seeks to do in his writing is akin to Paul's instruction to the Roman Christians to 'be transformed by the renewing of your mind. Then you will be able to test and approve what God's will is – his good, pleasing and perfect will' (Romans 12:2). John longs that his hearers (Revelation 1:3), and surely readers too, will no longer be captive to the status quo, but have their minds opened wide to the greater purposes of the creator and redeemer of the world. This is not about an escape into heaven or the future, but a new seeing and hearing of the truth of things on earth in the present such that our senses are changed forever.

Similarly, in the space between there is a unique opportunity for us to experience an 'unveiling' of what the world is really like and to gain fresh perspectives both on God and on ourselves. Just as

Revelation was written to comfort the afflicted as well as to afflict the comfortable, so the disruptive moments in our lives can cause us to seek both the consolation of God as well as his challenge where our lives have not been fully aligned with his purposes. One day we know that, through the coming again of Jesus Christ, he will make all things right, bringing justice and peace to the world at last. Such judgement – all too often misunderstood today as something nega- tive – gives unbounded hope for the situations of pain and heartache through which we must each journey. As Tom Wright expresses it:

> We need to remind ourselves that throughout the Bible, not least in the Psalms, God's coming judgement is a good thing, something to be celebrated, longed for, yearned over. It causes people to shout for joy, and indeed the trees of the field to clap their hands. In a world of systematic injustice, violence, bully- ing, arrogance and oppression, the thought that there might be a coming day when the wicked are finally put in their place and the poor and weak are given their due is the best news there can be. Faced with a world in rebellion, a world full of exploitation and wickedness, a good God must be a God of judgement.[11]

Therefore, whatever our situation, we know that a day is coming when all things will be made new: when God will be at home with his people at last; when he will wipe away every tear from our eyes; and when there will be no more death or mourning or crying or pain, because all these things belong to an alien age that is finally past. This is the hope that we proclaim and the hope by which we are sustained in the space between.

Sacred time – Epiphany

Epiphany is perhaps the least well-known season of the church year in much of the modern west. However, in the Christian east, it is the oldest feast next to Easter, or Pascha, and has always been cele- brated on 6 January. Epiphany means 'manifestation from above' or 'divine revelation'. An epiphany is a powerful religious experience: the moment when you suddenly understand something of deep importance. In the space between, we are crying out for such moments of epiphany – revelations in which sense is made of our experiences. The season of Epiphany invites us to take our micro-experiences of such longing and to place them within the macro-picture of God's revelation and manifestation to the world.

The family of Abraham was 'blessed in order to be a blessing' (see Genesis 12): through this nation that God would form from Abraham's seed, all the nations of the earth would know God's favour (the Gentiles or non-Jews). This call upon Israel carried the same temptation that it does for the people of God, the church, today – hoarding blessing, rather than passing it on; assuming that the gift is given because of special status rather than for the distinctive purpose of God in blessing the universal through the particular. Even in exile, Isaiah brought the prophetic reminder of Israel's vocation:

> [God] says, 'It is too small a thing for you to be my servant to restore the tribes of Jacob and bring back those of Israel I have kept. I will also make you a light for the Gentiles, that my salvation may reach to the ends of the earth.'
> ISAIAH 49:6

At the heart of God's work with Israel was his presence, a theme running through the whole of the Old Testament. Just think of God walking in the garden with Adam and Eve, the call of Abraham, Jacob at Bethel, and the ark of the covenant in the tabernacle and especially the temple. God's presence was what made Israel different and distinct from the other nations. The tragedy of exile, as revealed to the prophet Ezekiel (10:15–19), was the departure of that presence – the glory of God – from the temple. Even as a second temple was built, nowhere did the prophets say that the presence of God had returned. The end of exile could only come with the return of God's presence to the temple, which is exactly what John 1:14 celebrates:

> The Word became flesh and made his dwelling among us. We have seen his glory, the glory of the one and only Son, who came from the Father, full of grace and truth.

In Jesus Christ, the presence of God did return, such that the forgiveness of sins, which would always mark the end of exile, was now available. Israel's vocation was fulfilled through the one who was Israel-in-person and in him all the nations of the world are blessed. Epiphany is the revelation, the manifestation, of this wonderful truth.

Epiphany in the east originally commemorated the baptism of Christ. In some places, however, Jesus' birth, as well as some additional events from his life including his first miracle at Cana, were included in the celebration of Epiphany. It was only in the fourth century that the birth of Christ, first in the west and then in the east, began to be commemorated as a separate feast on 25 December. There is a difference of emphasis between east and west in the celebration of Epiphany. It might be said that the east emphasises the *vertical* dimension of Christ's revelation, while the west emphasises the *horizontal* dimension. Both dimensions are vital.

In the east, Epiphany focuses on the revelation of Christ as the Son of God, with God revealed as the Trinity of Father, Son and Holy Spirit. At his baptism (Matthew 3:13–17), Jesus sees an open heaven and the Spirit of God descending on him like a dove. He hears the voice of the Father, affirming his Sonship and expressing his Father's love for him and delight in him. I find it fascinating, given our modern elevation of Christmas, that in the early centuries of the church it was the baptism rather than the birth of Christ that was the focal point. This has logic to it as, in the words of St John Chrysostom, 'he was not manifested to all when he was born, but when he was baptised'.[12] I am challenged to place a higher emphasis on the baptism of Christ, which anticipates the baptism of the cross and paves the way for my own baptism. Through baptism, *we* also know an open heaven, receive the gift of the Spirit and hear the Father's love and delight for us as his children. Baptism is the place where our true identity is revealed.

In the west, Epiphany is primarily the manifestation of the divine Saviour Jesus Christ to the Gentiles and their acknowledgement of him as this. The double meaning is expressed by the way in which the western church has interpreted the offering of gold, frankincense and myrrh by the Magi. On the one hand, it saw these gifts as symbols of the three aspects of Christ's life – his coming as king, priest and prophet. On the other hand it re-enacted the offering in various ways by instituting appropriate acts of giving – to the poor, the church and the sick. As a non-Jew, this is where I come in on the story of God, following after the Magi. I'm also reminded of the blessing of giving myself away to others, even, or perhaps especially, when stuck in the space between.

Robert Webber suggests two ways to mark Epiphany, reflecting the vertical and horizontal focuses.[13] For the *vertical* dimension, he recommends a prayer, rooted in the east but with increasing appeal in the west, which seeks to locate us at home with God. It is called the Jesus Prayer and is drawn from Luke 18:13 – 'Lord Jesus Christ, Son of God, have mercy on me, a sinner.' The purpose of the prayer, prayed repeatedly and according to the rhythms of our breathing, is to fulfil Paul's mandate to 'pray continually' (1 Thessalonians 5:17). It is a prayer of words, though the goal is for it to become a prayer of the heart and so to establish constant communion with God. I have found this prayer to be a great blessing over the past decade since it was first introduced to me.[14]

For the *horizontal* dimension, Webber calls us to practise hospitality, with which God's presence is frequently associated in scripture. Perhaps the most well-known example of this is the hospitality that Abraham offers to three men who appear at the door of his tent (Genesis 18:1–15), and which inspired the famous icon of the Holy Trinity by Andrei Rublev. Webber shows how hospitality can challenge the exile of loneliness that so many experience:

> Hospitality evangelism is the kind of manifestation that may draw a stranger to the gospel into the very heart of Christ. The world is full of lonely people – students, singles, the disabled,

newcomers to town, the shy, the divorced, the aged, and the infirm. Like Abraham and Sarah we need to open up our homes and our lives to them, a hospitality that speaks volumes to the love and warmth of God.[15]

Sacred practice – pilgrimage

William Bridges writes:

> In other times and places, the person in transition left the village and went into an unfamiliar stretch of forest or desert. There the person would remain for a time, removed from the old connections, bereft of old identities, and stripped of the old reality. This was a time 'between dreams' in which fundamental chaos of the world's beginnings welled up and obliterated all forms. It was a place without a name – an empty space in the world and the lifetime where a new sense of the self could gestate.[16]

Without the same appreciation of the complexity of the space between, we struggle in modernity to find practices to live well within it. However, it is interesting that, as much as we may fail to always understand it, there is something intuitive in how we behave at such times. People in transition, perhaps without quite knowing why, often sense the need to be alone and away from life as usual. Maybe we process this as a need for 'thinking time'. Nonetheless, time out, in a different place from usual, is something we naturally seem to appreciate as being good for us.

Looking back on my own life, I'm interested to observe that this was what Sarah and I did when we were struggling to conceive. Sarah's boss at the time suggested that we spend a few days at Easter on Lindisfarne, Holy Island, and though we knew something of the story of the place, neither of us had visited there before. The thought of making pilgrimage given our low-church backgrounds was entirely novel and perhaps even a little suspicious. 'You can pray to God anywhere' would have been the voice in our heads, making place only an insignificant detail and, in retrospect, reducing prayer merely to the spiritual rather than something that is always embodied. We had heard talk of 'thin places', though again, on first listen, this seemed questionable. How can one place be more 'holy' than another, when God is omnipresent?

The journey from our home at this time in Leeds to Lindisfarne was meaningful in a way that we would never have expected. The leaving felt weighted with significance which instinctively called us to say a prayer together to mark the moment. The music playing in the car, the conversation, the views on the way – these were all ordinary yet somehow different. We both carried a sense of expectation, though we didn't quite know for what. Martin Robinson observes: 'Many set off on pilgrimage with little concept of what the interior journey might mean and meet themselves en route in surprising and sometimes disturbing ways.'[17] On pilgrimage, it is the journey as much as the destination that is significant.

We were on Holy Island for just a few days, yet it somehow felt like an eternity. The wonder of the island, with its tidal rhythm that twice each day leaves it disconnected from the mainland, spoke profound wisdom to us of the daily rhythms of prayer that we needed to cultivate. We loved the moments when tourists would leave the island and it would become deserted again – offering us the time and space that we needed as pilgrims.

We learned new ways to pray. The Celtic Daily Prayer of the Northumbria Community became very precious to us, and remains so more than 15 years later. Such set prayer would again have been frowned upon by us before this time as being 'religious'. Yet, in our pain, we had run short of words. We found new life in articulating language that others had crafted with such beauty, and this began to enable channels of connection with God to be opened up again.

Most of all, we came to a place of surrender. Surely this is our primary need in the space between. We recognised that we had to give in, and to give up the struggle in which we had recently been engaged. We came to see that we had to let go of our dreams as they were, as they had become a torment to us. We had to lose control, or to recognise that we had never had as much control as we might have hoped for in the first place. This was a time of tears and of breaking. It felt that we had been reduced to nothing. Yet the act of surrender lifted a weight from us. The journey home was somehow lighter. Though our circumstances had not changed, it felt as though the world was a different place to inhabit. This is not to say that we were complete in our surrender. However, without that encounter, we would have continued to spiral downwards in ways that were unhealthy.

Many years on, I'm interested to understand a little more of why that experience was so profound for us and why it resonated so deeply within us. It seems to me that pilgrimage is the intentional practice of exile. Going to a place that is not our own, that is alien to us, mirrors externally the internal reality of our hearts in the space between. We go to an unknown place because we feel like we're in an unknown place.[18] Frédéric Gros is in agreement:

> The primary meaning of *peregrines* is foreigner or exile. The pilgrim, originally, is not one who is heading somewhere (Rome, Jerusalem, etc.), but essentially one who is not at home where he is walking… he's a stranger, a foreigner.[19]

On pilgrimage, the new horizons that open up for us in location also unveil fresh vistas for our soul – even if nothing changes in our circumstances. Somehow, we gain a new perspective on reality. We so often define life according to our external situations, yet exile and pilgrimage invite us to see things more creatively than this. In the place of surrender to God, reality feels greatly expanded and new possibilities emerge. Just as we locate ourselves physically by landmarks, so it is that pilgrimage alerts us to new landmarks of the soul. As in Alfred Korzybski's celebrated aphorism, 'the map is not the territory' – you have to go there to understand it.

Sacred stories

Historical saints – Ignatius of Loyola and Jackie Pullinger

Mark Sayers retells a scene from a David Attenborough documentary. It is set in a cave, deep in the jungle. The cave has highly corrosive acid running through it, which, together with the lack of light and dank conditions, might lead one to assume that no life form could ever live there. However, Attenborough observes that certain life forms not only survive but, in fact, thrive here. They are known as 'extremophiles' – a term that covers a wide degree of species able to exist in extreme temperatures, live at great depth of sea or exist in arid deserts.[20] In the same way, Margaret Wheatley observes that even in the most caustic and dysfunctional workplaces, a certain kind of person and leader can be found.[21] They are not affected by their environments; rather, they have an ability to draw their sense of meaning from *outside of them*.

Such people are not born, but formed. The British historian Arnold J. Toynbee has termed this formational process 'withdrawal-and-return'.[22] Sayers argues that God deliberately takes people through such a process in order to shape their inner world in the 'withdrawal' phase. Here, they discover something of a 'cultural key' that can then be brought back in the 'return' phase to offer life and healing to others.[23] A good example of this is Ignatius of Loyola – a man whose life, perhaps not unlike our own, did not turn out as he expected it to.

Ignatius of Loyola
Ignatius was a soldier and a bit of a playboy. He dreamed of a life of military glory; however, his dreams were shattered, instantly and violently, by a cannonball that left him disabled. His impediment led him on a long journey towards total submission to God, eventually sending him on pilgrimage to Jerusalem.

Ignatius' wanderings would land him in the small Spanish town of Manresa. He hadn't intended to stay there long, yet a combination of illnesses and powerful encounters with God meant that he stayed there for a year. Ignatius had always been someone who had enjoyed all the trappings of worldly success. Yet here in a cave in Manresa, through isolation, prayer and illness, God had other plans for his life, and Ignatius would slowly arrive at a place of surrender. The experience of exile offered Ignatius a profound opportunity for greater self-understanding – time to think through who he really was and who he really wanted to be. This gave him the grace to look upon himself all the way down, with all of his flaws, which brought him to a place of greater humility. Ignatius' experience of injury, illness and isolation enabled him to gain a distance from the cultural narratives he'd always been surrounded by and enveloped within, and to break the hold that these had on him. He was forced to learn dependence on God. In this, Ignatius seems to have been able to grasp his sense of gifting far more securely when he left Manresa than when he'd arrived.

It's interesting that God still made use of the best of the earlier part of Ignatius' life. His military background, for example, would shape the discipline and organisation that he would instil in the Jesuits; his diplomatic abilities, learned on the edges of courtly life, would help him to engage key leaders in the growth of the order; and his intellectual training would aid his writing in ways that continue to impact people today. These are all examples of what J. Robert Clinton calls 'sovereign foundations'[24] – the manner in which God uses our family, environmental and historical backgrounds to shape us for the future in ways we are not able to recognise at the time.

Ignatius was profoundly changed at Manresa. The experience of withdrawal reshaped him. Out of this came something that has benefited the lives of millions of people, myself included – what came to be known as the *Spiritual Exercises*. This was a kind of workbook for a deepening life in God, based on withdrawal and return, and it is one of the most-read Christian books in history. Ignatius could not stay in the cave at Manresa forever, though – he had to return to the world outside, and his exercises were the powerful fruit of this homecoming.

Jackie Pullinger, on the other hand, set out for an unfamiliar land and has remained there ever since.

Jackie Pullinger

The apocryphal story is told of Hernán Cortés, who in 1519 led a large expedition to Mexico. The goal was to capture magnificent treasure that was said to be held there. Dramatically, Cortés destroyed his ships upon arrival. This sent a clear message to his men: 'There is no turning back: we will either win, or we will perish.' Within two years, Cortés and his men had conquered the Aztec Empire. Jackie Pullinger has spent her life doing something of the Christian missionary equivalent of this. Pullinger's life is one of seeking disruption and exile rather than it being thrust upon her. Her story is famously told in *Chasing the Dragon*, which I remember being gripped by when I was a child and which my eldest daughter is now enjoying herself. Without question, however, Pullinger would reject the label 'exile'. I imagine her response would be that there is no such thing as withdrawal and return, only to be obedient to God's leading wherever this may take you.

In her early 20s, having graduated from the Royal College of Music in London, Jackie wished to become an overseas missionary. However, she was unable to gain support from the mission organisations that she wrote to. She then received some radical advice from a minister: 'Buy a ticket for a boat as far as you can get and pray to know when to get off the boat!' A dream brought Hong Kong to her mind, and so in 1966 she travelled by boat, not knowing anyone there and with only £10 to her name. She was allowed into the region only because her mother's godson was a police officer there.

Pullinger's life in Hong Kong began in Kowloon Walled City, a lawless slum full of opium dens, pornographic film theatres and triads who profited from crime and prostitution. It was a place of very deep darkness. She found work as a primary school teacher and got to know some of the gang members and leaders, and as she started her work of loving the unlovable, she witnessed incredible breakthrough. Heroin users would pray in tongues and find themselves miraculously released from their addiction; crime bosses surrendered their lives to Jesus; prostitutes quit their work. Pullinger also established a youth centre that helped the drug addicts and street sleepers inside the city. The Walled City may have been demolished and replaced with a park in the mid-1990s, but Pullinger's work among Hong Kong's poorest continues to this day through the organisation she founded, the St Stephen's Society.[25]

Pullinger's life message is simple and transformational: get yourself sure enough of God's love that you can go out and share it with the lost. She is undoubtedly a formidable character and has a straightforward approach to following Jesus. 'I had no preconceptions,' she says. 'I just thought this was an adventure and I was going to go wherever God took me and share Jesus along the way. And that's really the adventure I'm still on.'[26] She refuses the tag of having a 'ministry', saying that she simply has a life in which the joy is knowing Jesus. She believes that every Christian is called to the poor.

Jackie Pullinger has radically embraced disruption and liminality, not as a season, but an entire way of life.

Contemporary saint

This is the story, in their own words, of a friend who has journeyed, or is still journeying, through the space between.

If you speak to any gardener, they will tell you that the process of uprooting a plant and replanting it is often a delicate and painful process for the plant and sometimes also for the gardener. For a plant to be replanted, it has to leave its old soil – in which it has put its roots down deep – leave the familiar, warm and comfortable and move into a different environment, which can feel cold, uninhabitable, unfamiliar and rootless. I am assured by many gardening experts that these uprooted plants can survive and thrive if cared for properly. The root system of the plant must be re-established effectively in order for the plant to grow and thrive.

This understanding of plants has really helped me make sense of a time in our lives when we went through our own experience of being uprooted. This feeling of being uprooted was our own exile, a leaving of our home and following God's call where nothing felt familiar, predictable or safe. I can only describe our own time of exile as incredibly painful, disorientating and lonely. There was nothing comforting about it, no signposts we recognised, no memories we could draw upon, no familiar faces we could take comfort in, no special places or landmarks we could make reference to. Everything shouted to me of the loss of what we had left behind and the deep void now in our lives. My heart ached to go home and not to feel this sense of loss and grief as to all we had left behind. Just like the natural process of uprooting and replanting, moving your family and setting up a new home is a long and delicate process that needs navigating carefully and tenderly.

How do we draw on God during these times? How do we find peace and rest and navigate the mixture of emotions and feelings, when everything around us feels strange, empty and unfamiliar? I had to remind myself that God does not call us as his followers to a life of comfort, warmth and ease. We may have our own struggles and difficulties, but he has promised to always be with us. I remember being told countless times when I was younger that it may be costly following Jesus, and it certainly felt that way. He calls us to follow him even when we can't see the way ahead clearly, and even when it doesn't quite work out as you imagine it.

A plant needs roots: roots that go down deep into the soil, which becomes home for the plant. We need roots: roots that not only firmly establish us in God's love but also in the place where he has asked us to serve him. It is these roots that help strengthen us and help us to grow. Would I have chosen to go through our time in exile? No, probably not. But I know that through it I have learnt more about God, myself and my family.

So what have I learnt through our experience of exile and replanting? I have learnt that our roots are essential to our survival, and it takes time for them to be re-established in different soil. It may need more tending and care for a time, but the plant will be able to grow stronger and taller. Years on, we are all flourishing in different ways. My life may look different to what I'd imagined, but I am genuinely thankful to God and his faithfulness through it all. I have been reminded that prayer is a lifeline, but it does not always provide us with a quick-fix solution to some of our struggles. Prayer sustains us and helps us persevere, to dig in and dig deep. I have learnt that we need friends to help us on our journey and that they are truly a gift from God. I have learnt that we can trust God to look after our children, even when our plan is different to his for them. We must follow God's call for our lives, even if it makes us feel uncomfortable and disorientated, because it is in precisely these testing times that we grow and are transformed forever.

The love from which we can never be exiled

Who shall separate us from the love of Christ? Shall trouble or hardship or persecution or famine or nakedness or danger or sword? As it is written:

'For your sake we face death all day long;
    we are considered as sheep to be slaughtered.'

No, in all these things we are more than conquerors through him who loved us. For I am convinced that neither death nor life, neither angels nor demons, neither the present nor the future, nor any powers, neither height nor depth, nor anything else in all creation, will be able to separate us from the love of God that is in Christ Jesus our Lord.
ROMANS 8:35–39

Questions for reflection

1 Where/what/who is 'home' for you? Give thanks for the gift of home.
2 When have you known experiences of exile in your life? What did they teach you?
3 What in this chapter gives you most hope for living in a season of exile?

5

The wilderness: when life is stripped back

You, God, are my God, earnestly I seek you; I thirst for you, my whole being longs for you, in a dry and parched land where there is no water.
PSALM 63:1

In scripture and in life, the school for discipleship is the desert rather than the oasis.[1]

Human emotions – barrenness and emptiness

The image of wandering in the desert powerfully captures our experience of life in times of emptiness, being stripped back to the bone, running dry. The wilderness stands for the place of vast, almost overwhelming, barrenness. It's where nourishment has become scarce and all sources of water have run out. In the Bible, the wilderness or desert is a 'remote place' (see Leviticus 16:22), a land of constant struggle and fight, and the ultimate territory of death due to lack of sustenance and vegetation. The wilderness is a void; a wasteland. Life has no luxury left within it, and has merely become a place of survival. The desert is clearly not the place for permanent residence. The deserts of the Middle East are vast and hot and dry. They are lonely, uninhabited. One goes to the desert in order to get *through* it, not to stop off there.

On a trip to the Holy Land a number of years ago, however, this is exactly what we did in the wilderness of Judea. We got off the coach and were invited to find our own space in this vast, desolate setting. While the Judean desert may be one of the world's smallest desert regions, we were not lacking in our ability to spread out. We spent an hour by ourselves, sat in the midst of such barrenness. It was an experience such as I've never had before or since. It was almost over-whelmingly empty – there was nothing to do, nothing really to look at, beyond the vast sameness of all that was around.

Sat in the sand that day, I found the experience deeply uncomfortable. Blaise Pascal, who died young at the age of 39 having made huge contributions to physics and mathematics, geometry and probability, famously said: 'All of humanity's problems stem from man's inability to sit quietly in a room alone.' Yet, in the desert, time seemed to slow to a standstill. Minutes felt like hours. With nothing outward to behold, the only place to look was inward, and herein lies the source of the discomfort that the wilderness brings. In the desert, we are faced with ourselves. Everything is stripped back to the core, and there is only us and God. The barren place can expose the void within us, hence the need to avoid, distract or defend at all costs. Many die in the desert. In this way, it might be seen as nothing but a large cemetery that can bury us.

Yet there is another angle on the desert. 'What makes the desert beau-tiful,' said the little prince, 'is that somewhere it hides a well.'[2] Streams of living water can flow, even in the driest of locations. For many, the desert can be an unlikely setting for new birth. The episode described in chapter 2 of the battle between Jacob and the angel occurred in the desert (Genesis 32:24). The prophet Hosea beautifully describes the wilderness as the place in which God, the tender lover, allures and woos his people, longing to draw them into intimacy with him again. Against all expectations, the desolate place is a site of God's concen-trated presence. Moses, David and many other of Israel's great leaders spent time there. Elijah made the desert's burning sands his home, only periodically emerging to challenge King Ahab to repentance.

John the Baptist, with heavy overtones of Elijah, prepared the way for Jesus from the desert. Willingly or unwillingly, the desert can lead us to God. In fact, more than this, 'the Scriptures teach us that there is no path to God that does not pass through the wilderness. The God of the Bible is the God of the desert.'[3] Mark Ireland and Mike Booker continue, 'There is something about the unforgiving landscape of the desert, where danger is never far away, that forces us to do serious business with God. In Scripture and in life, the school for discipleship is the desert rather than the oasis.'[4]

Sacred scriptures

Old Testament – Israel in the wilderness

The archetypal experience of the desert in the scriptures is the 40 years that the people of Israel spent wandering in the wastelands, led and comforted by God, before they finally gained redemption in the promised land. We observed that the desert is not a place you stop off at but one you go through. Once freed from their slavery to Egypt, it took the people of Israel seven days to cross the Red Sea, breaking completely clear of Egyptian control. It should have taken them only another eleven days or so to reach the promised land. Yet, somehow, Israel walked those few hundred miles that remained for *forty years*. We noted that the desert can bury people, and it certainly did for Israel as every man of war numbered in the first census after leaving Egypt – with the notable exceptions of Joshua and Caleb – died in this period without reaching the promised land. So, what went wrong?

God had promised Abraham a land, the land of Canaan, from which his family would grow to be a blessing to the nations. Moses, Israel's leader in the exodus, asked for a reconnaissance mission to take place to assess the geography of the land, the strength and numbers of the population, the potential of the land for agriculture, its civic organisation and its forestry conditions. The twelve spies sent out to fulfil this request, one from each of the tribes of Israel, were asked to be positive in their outlook and to return with samples of local produce.

However, when the spies returned they were full of despair. The land flowed 'with milk and honey' and they brought back some of its fruit, yet they were completely overwhelmed as to Israel's chances of ever inheriting it, in spite of God's promise. The report was factual but faithless – it focused on the strength of the people and the fortification of their towns, without any regard for the God who was bigger than all things. Caleb, a man of faith, saw things differently, yet the ten spies doubled down on their pessimism, moving from faithless negativity to fatalistic defeatism – 'We are not able to go up against this people, for they are stronger than we are'; 'To ourselves we seemed like grasshoppers, and so we seemed to them' (see Numbers 13:26–33).

Israel's protest escalated as they raised a loud cry and wept through the night. With warped perspective, they began to see themselves as better off under the oppression of Egypt than walking God's path to freedom through the wilderness. It's amazing how strong the urge to leave a time of disruption can be that we might be willing to trade it for seemingly *any* form of certainty. Israel's knee-jerk plan was to install a new leader and to head back to the 'security' of the land of brutality, oppression and slavery. God's judgement came, the leaders of faith interceded and there was forgiveness – yet Israel would have to wander the desert until all except Joshua and Caleb had died in it. In this, they received the fate that they had set for themselves.

It's often been said that the easy task was to get Israel out of Egypt – the far harder job was to get Egypt out of Israel. We so often imagine that, if only we could change the *outward* circumstances of our lives, then all would be well. It can take a long time for it to dawn on us, at least it has for me, that we still carry around with us all of our past, unless we choose to process it with God and others and to find healing from it. In the wise words of Richard Rohr, 'If you don't transform your suffering, you'll transmit it.' This is an issue of our mindset, of the lenses through which we view the world. Mindsets are so powerful because so often we don't even realise that they are there.

In Egypt, over the course of 400 years, Israel had developed the mindset of slaves – rather than the children of God that they were redeemed to be. They had been oppressed and beaten down, and this had powerfully affected the way in which they viewed God and saw the world. To Israel's vision, the world was big, powerful and scary, while God was small and inadequate in comparison. It was as though they were looking the wrong way down a telescope, to magnify what should be diminished and diminish what should be magnified. Even a mighty act of redemption, like the exodus, was not enough to undo 400 years of such formation. A process of counter-formation in the wilderness would be required, and, given how slow to learn we can be ourselves, perhaps the wonder is that this only took 40 years.

People with the mindset of slaves see the world as a place of scarcity: there is never enough, and the only suitable response is to grumble and complain. The grumbling may often be nonsensical, but this only goes to show how powerfully mindsets have been shaped. Thus Israel's farcical hunger pangs for cucumbers (Numbers 11:5), as well as other haute cuisine from the menus of Egypt, demonstrated a recasting of slavery as pure freedom in ways that are only warped. In the desert, God was asking Israel to grow up, to take responsibility for themselves before him. Those who have been oppressed sometimes struggle to do this. Often it is easier to remain in the familiarity of slavery and victimhood than to walk the long and unfamiliar path to freedom. Israel were no longer slaves, they were the free children of God. Yet with such freedom comes responsibility and the call to grow into maturity.

I've come to recognise this mindset of scarcity in myself. It's taken me a long time to become properly aware of it and to recognise its scale and hold on me. Exploring how insignificance, fear, condemnation and rejection can all play their parts in the development of a critical spirit is a vital first step of the process, I've found. Yet the journey beyond this is hard. Choosing new patterns and embracing new mindsets takes time, and it needs the support of a loving community around us. I'm convinced that we can only ever be loved, not forced, into freedom. We may also need the skill and attention of professionals, and through counselling I for one have found a freedom to move beyond the past that I never thought I would have.

There is an intentional practice that takes us beyond a mindset of scarcity – praise and thanksgiving. The benefits of gratitude are increasingly well known as a habit of wellness and productivity; however, the object of our appreciation is also of vital importance. In Deuteronomy 8, Israel were reminded that, when they had come into the land of promise and had eaten and were satisfied, they should praise the Lord for all that he had given them (v. 10). Moses could see that a season of comfort always brings with it the danger of complacency and forgetting God's goodness. For this reason, the emptiness of the desert is the ideal place to learn to be grateful. It is the experience of many that we become the most thankful in our lives at exactly the point when things are stripped away from us, for only then do we see all that we have been given. Thanksgiving is the antidote to a scarcity mindset, as it focuses our hearts on the abundance that we have been given in Christ. Praise draws our minds to the wonder and grandeur of God – Father, Son and Holy Spirit – and causes us to place ourselves and the issues in our lives within their true perspective. Praise and thanksgiving are a vital way to begin each of our days, so as to set them out on the right course, as well as to bring them to a close.

Israel might have been thankful, not full of grumbling, as God spread a table for her in the wilderness, in the words of Psalm 78:19. Water was provided, manna and quail given, to sustain her through her desert wanderings. Yet Israel's hunger in the desert was a deep source of humbling (Deuteronomy 8:2–3), used by God to strip her back and to reveal the idols that were in her heart. Even God's provision was designed to create proper dependence on him – manna given daily (except on the sabbath) with an instruction and prohibition not to hoard so as to keep Israel reliant on the source. As Christians, we inhabit a similar practice when we pray, 'Give us today our daily bread.' Conscious of our need, we come afresh each day to the one who alone can provide.

The tribes of Israel truly became the people of God in the desert, for it was there that they came to know God and his ways more fully. For us, it seems there are some lessons that can only be learned in the wilderness, where our identity as his children is more fully inhabited. Though it may take longer than we'd expected, we can trust that God *will* lead us through our desert seasons to the places of promise that he has for us, and that he will abundantly provide for us along the way.

Psalm 63

The psalm that speaks most obviously of the wilderness is Psalm 63. It is introduced as a psalm of David when he was in the desert of Judah, and invites us to consider two desert seasons in the life of David: the first, when he fled to the wilderness from Saul (1 Samuel 22—25) and the second when he ran from his son Absalom (2 Samuel 15—17). In both cases, David's life is on the line and the desert is a temporary place of refuge for him from those who seek his life. David can live with the frustration and ache of present circumstances because the God he has encountered in the past in Jerusalem is the same God he knows in the wilderness in the present. He finds encouragement in the psalm by looking back and looking forward. In the space between, we always find ourselves looking both ways.

Psalm 63 has been identified by some as another lament psalm. These psalms normally stem from a perception that God is absent, distant and unresponsive. They usually have a petition or plea to God for some form of deliverance. However, this psalm is quite different. While enemies are identified (vv. 9–10), they do not seem to be foremost in the psalmist's mind. Instead, it is God's presence that is front and centre. As a result, some have considered this to be a song of trust or a song of confidence. The structure of Psalm 63 is unclear, and it has been explored in a variety of ways. We'll look at it here in four sections: verses 1–2, which speak of longing and encounter; verses 3–5, which tell of celebration; verses 6–8, which express trust in God and commitment to him; and verses 9–11, which look to a confident future hope.

The psalm is founded upon the personal relationship we saw Jacob discover at Bethel – 'You, God, are my God' (v. 1). The opening two verses introduce the theme of the psalm. The metaphor of the desert provides the context of a desperate seeking, thirsting and longing after God. This isn't a merely spiritual enterprise but something that consumes the psalmist's entire being. Such longing takes place because of what's happened in the past. The psalmist, in verse 2, can look back to a time of encounter with God – in the sanctuary, the temple in Jerusalem – when God's power and glory were known. This may be past tense for now, but there is the hope that it can become present tense again. In this way, the seeking of the start of this section becomes a seeing by the end.

The unquenchable longing for God and the celebratory remembering of past encounters lead to a declared intention to praise God again. God's love is better even than life itself, which the psalmist is sure will lead to lips that glorify God, praise which is lifelong and hands that are lifted in God's name. This exuberant response will come because of the deep pleasure the psalmist anticipates from the encounter, likened to a sumptuous feast in which every hint of hunger is satisfied. It's as though those previous encounters with God have been so transformative that they remain in the muscle memory, even within the desert. The psalmist's keen anticipation of another such encounter, becomes the answer to the longing of verse 1.

In verses 6–8, the exuberance of the previous section gives way to a mood of deep trust, as a future focus transitions to a recalling of the past. God is remembered and meditated upon in activities that speak of devotion and commitment. God's help leads to a shouting for joy under God's protection – his 'wings'. There has been a clinging, cleaving, sticking to God (the word is difficult to translate but speaks of inseparable devotion) because of the divine upholding of the psalmist.

No wonder there is such confidence for the future, against all the odds, in verses 9–11. There is a contrast between what will happen to the psalmist's enemies and what will happen to the king. The former will be destroyed – going down to the depths, being given to the sword and becoming food for jackals. The latter, however, will rejoice in God. Meanwhile, the community of faith will rejoice, while the mouths of liars will be silenced. Read Christologically, this king is Jesus Christ, who on the cross said, 'I am thirsty,' and who was pierced that streams of living water might flow from his side to cover the dry and parched ground where there is no water (John 19:28, 34).

The psalm has a distinctive contribution to offer for those living in the space between. It teaches us to look both backwards and forwards for our encouragement. We must look back to times of past encounter when we have seen God and beheld his power and glory, as well as when God has proved to be our deliverer, protector and supporter. We should take note of these times – even using the lull to record something of our life with God to this point and those encounters with him that we are able to celebrate. As well as looking back, we look forward to being in such a place of encounter again, and can anticipate it in the conviction that God's commitment to us does not change.

However, what the psalmist prizes above all else – beyond deliverance, protection or support – is the very presence of God himself. This presence is the ultimate end of Psalm 63. Everything else fades to the background; only this can truly satisfy. Even when it seems to be gone in the present, it can be remembered from the past and hoped for again for the future.

Jesus Christ – the wilderness

Jesus Christ was familiar with the desert place. 'Desert' in its widest sense doesn't only stand for places of sand and heat – the Greek word *eremos* has a wide variety of meanings, such as a wilderness, a deserted or desolate place, and a solitary or quiet place.

It's interesting to observe that the first thing Jesus does after the launch of his public ministry – having had to wait 30 years for this to begin – is to head into the desert. In the gospels of Matthew and

Luke, Jesus is 'led by the Spirit into the wilderness' (Matthew 4:1; Luke 4:1). Mark is stronger – 'At once the Spirit sent him out into the wilderness' (Mark 1:12) – which gives the impression of an irresistible force propelling, even expelling, Jesus there. Jesus goes into the desert to be tempted by the devil, or the 'satan' (the 'accuser' or 'adversary'). His preparation for such an encounter was to fast for 40 days, which left him famished. For a long time, I misunderstood this story. It felt illogical to me that Jesus would take on the devil from a place of weakness – in the desert, alone and starving. It took a while for me to comprehend that, in the words of John Mark Comer, 'the wilderness isn't the place of weakness; it's the place of strength'. Comer goes on:

> Jesus was led by the Spirit into the wilderness because it was there, and only there, that Jesus was at the height of his spiritual powers. It was only after a month and a half of prayer and fasting in the quiet place that he had the capacity to take on the devil himself and walk away unscathed.[5]

In this place, Jesus is tempted, just as we are (Hebrews 4:15), with temptations that cut to the core of who he is. His sense of being loved and called has just been affirmed by the Father at his baptism, and straight away this is undermined, explicitly so in the first two temptations. Satisfy your appetite. Demonstrate how impressive you are. Fulfil your ambition here and now. Jesus resists the lure of such temptations by drawing on scripture embedded deep within him. He isn't quoting proof texts like the devil; instead, he understands their place within Israel's own journey through the wilderness, with his 40 days atoning for their 40 years. He is the true Israel in person. Moreover, behind this story is the even wider horizon of Adam and Eve, with Jesus saying 'no' where the first couple could not, for he is the true human being, embracing the way of the cross from the beginning.

The fruit of this encounter is shown by the contrast between Luke's description of Jesus at the beginning and the end of the episode. Jesus goes into the desert 'full of the Holy Spirit' but comes out 'in the power of the Spirit' (Luke 4:1, 14). As Mike Pilavachi has said, 'The spiritual equation is this: filled with the Spirit plus led by the Spirit into the desert equals returning in the power of the Spirit.'[6] Perhaps this casts a new light on our own wilderness experiences. We often see the desert as only dry and barren, a place of weakness; yet the kingdom of God turns the world on its head. Weakness is strength. Emptiness is fullness. Growth comes by subtraction. This is all so counter-intuitive that we can struggle to comprehend it.

Jesus said that his sheep hear his voice (John 10:27). However, the 'gentle whisper' that Elijah heard on Mount Horeb (1 Kings 19:12) cannot be heard in the permanent noise and chattering of everyday life. In the same way, John the Baptist retreated to the desert of Judea to become the 'voice of one calling in the wilderness' (John 1:23). And here, Jesus, following the words of Isaiah, also went to the wilderness before his public exhortation to 'prepare the way for the Lord; make straight in the desert a highway for our God' (Isaiah 40:3). The wilderness, being a no man's land, offers a unique opportunity for encounter with God – an opportunity that is scarcely available amid the hustle and bustle of life-as-normal.

No wonder that Jesus, time and time again, actively sought out the deserted place:

> Very early in the morning, while it was still dark, Jesus got up, left the house and went off to a solitary place, where he prayed.
> MARK 1:35

> Yet the news about him spread all the more, so that crowds of people came to hear him and to be healed of their illnesses. But Jesus often withdrew to lonely places and prayed.
> LUKE 5:15–16

This leads us into the most well-known of all of Jesus' miracles.

New Testament – the feeding of the 5,000

The story of the feeding of the 5,000 is one of the few events in the life of Jesus to appear in all four gospels (Matthew 14:13–21; Mark 6:31–44; Luke 9:12–17; John 6:1–14). Jesus has beckoned the disciples away from the crowd and towards 'a solitary place' to rest. The people of Israel were forced into the desert because of their disobedience. Here Jesus is asking his disciples to choose the barren location as a means of spiritual renewal. The disciples are being pressed upon with no time even to eat, so they take a boat out and choose to embrace the wilderness. Yet their retreat will not last long. They are quickly spotted and the crowd arrives ahead of them. Their solitary place has been invaded.

I love this passage because it plays with my categories around boundaries. People-pleasers can fail to impose sufficient boundaries, such that they allow others to flood in and overrun their priorities. Over-firm boundary-setters can fix boundaries that are so impermeable they don't let people in. Many of us find ourselves caught at both extremes. However, Jesus is different. He isn't obsessed with boundaries, soft or hard; instead, he's moved by the Father's compassion – that gut-wrenching feeling for people in the depths of his being.

Jesus recognises that the desert is a place of learning, and so he teaches a crowd who are desperate. For the disciples, their learning will be more practical. The problem of hungry people is obvious to them, though their solution is to send everyone away to buy something. Jesus has a different idea: 'You give them something to eat.' The disciples are baffled and overwhelmed – such a plan would be absurdly expensive as well as logistically impossible given the size of the crowd. Their responses are logical yet lacking in faith, contingent on human understanding not divine possibility. In the desert, it can feel as though we have so little resource available that nothing can be done through it. The error in such an equation is that we factor out the one who works miracles of multiplication.

'How many loaves do you have?' Jesus asks. All that the disciples can gather is five loaves and two fish – which John's gospel tells us has come from a boy's packed lunch. How revealing that while the adults compute the human impossibility of the scenario, the child simply offers what he has, trusting that it will somehow be enough. The desert teaches us to grow up for sure, but never to lose that childlike faith and dependence that Jesus was, and is, so drawn to. Responsibility and reliance together are what we need.

So it is that Jesus sits people down in groups. Mark has the wonderful extra detail of 'green grass', a symbol of life and hope in the desolate place. Jesus takes what's been offered, gives thanks, breaks the loaves and gives them to the disciples to set before the people, before dividing the two fish among them as well. Beautifully, everyone eats and is filled, and there is much left over. In the place where everything is stripped back, we give the little that we have. Amazingly this will always be enough. Nothing more is required. Jesus does the rest. Truly, he can be relied upon to spread a table for us in the wilderness.

> *The Lord is my shepherd, I lack nothing.*
> * He makes me lie down in green pastures,*
> *he leads me beside quiet waters,*
> * he refreshes my soul.*
> *He guides me along the right paths*
> * for his name's sake....*
> *You prepare a table before me*
> * in the presence of my enemies.*
> *You anoint my head with oil;*
> * my cup overflows.*
> *Surely your goodness and love will follow me*
> * all the days of my life,*
> *and I will dwell in the house of the Lord forever.*
> PSALM 23:1–3, 5–6

Sacred time – Lent

The season of Lent is a wilderness period of 40 days to prepare for Easter, and to consider what it means to follow Christ on the way to the cross. The English word 'Lent' is a shortened form of the Old English word *lencten*, meaning 'spring season'. Literally, it denotes the lengthening of days as the sun's light lingers in the sky. Culturally today, the heart of Lent has been hollowed out so as to become focused either on giving things up, particularly the 'naughty but nice' stuff like alcohol or chocolate, or taking things up, often good, general habits. Yet where there is no Godward focus, Lent is reduced to an exercise in individual willpower – simply another means of self-improvement. However, Lent is an invitation into the wilderness to encounter Christ. The purpose of Lent might be summed up in the words of that desert-dweller John the Baptist: 'He must become greater; I must become less' (John 3:30). Chaplain Mike puts it more bluntly: 'Lent is not about getting better. Lent is about preparing to die'.[7] This accords with the fact that the Lenten season is traditionally the time when catechumens are prepared for baptism – 40 days of getting ready to drown. Thomas Merton writes:

> God's people first came into existence when the children of Israel were delivered from slavery in Egypt and called out into the desert to be educated into freedom, to learn to live with no other master but God himself.[8]

Merton's words sum up the true purpose of Lent. God longs to draw us into the freedom of following him – Father, Son and Holy Spirit – with all of our heart, mind, soul and strength. The desert of Lent is the place in which our idolatries are exposed. With everything stripped back, we come to see what it is that we truly rely upon to live. We may call God our Lord, but functionally we can live under the rule of other masters. We may have left Egypt, yet Egypt may not have left us. Lent is the time in which our false gods are seen for what they are, and there is a turning back to the true God. It's only the desert, which strips us back, that can make this possible.

In this season, says Christine Sine, God wants:

> … to liberate us from the bondages of our slavery to self-centredness, greed, busyness, and rampant consumerism. God wants us to help others be liberated from the bondages of poverty, sex trafficking, imprisonment, addictions, injustice and disease. And God wants us to commit to the liberation of our earth from pollution, deforestation and species extinction.[9]

The beginning of Lent is Ash Wednesday. This wasn't marked in the tradition of church in which I grew up, but is something, as with the other seasons of the church's calendar, that I have come to value for the way it orients me in the story of Christ and forms the life of Christ in me. The 40 days of Lent mirror the 40 days of Christ in the wilderness. The scriptures for the day spotlight a returning to God (Joel 2:1–2, 12–17), a crying out for mercy and restoration (Psalm 51) and an assurance of forgiveness (John 8:1–11). The central act is the imposition of ashes on the forehead, with the powerful reminder: 'Remember that you are dust, and to dust you shall return.' These are desert words, that cut back any pretence or facade we might put up as to who we really are.

Lent is not a humanist endeavour of self-improvement and it cannot be done apart from Christ. In C.S. Lewis' Narnia story, *The Voyage of the Dawn Treader*, Eustace comes into the possession of a dragon's treasure, but in reality the treasure comes to possess him. 'Sleeping on a Dragon's hoard with greedy dragonish thoughts in his heart,' the story says, 'he had become a dragon himself.'[10] Eustace is shocked to wake up to discover scales in place of his skin. He finds himself in pain and weeps for what he has become. How will he become free again? Almost in a dream, Eustace is drawn by the lion, Aslan – the Christ character – to a garden where there is a well. He is told to bathe, but first he must 'undress'. Eustace tries to, scratching off his scales, peeling off more and more of his dragon's skin; yet in spite of all that is removed, he keeps finding further layers underneath. 'How ever many skins have I got to take off?',[11] Eustace asks himself. The reply comes from Aslan, 'You will have to let me undress you'. Eustace said that the Lion's claws cut so deeply that 'the hurt is worse than anything I've ever felt'. But the Dragon skin is at last peeled off completely, and the Lion throws Eustace into the well and dresses him – an incredible image of baptism in which Christ cleanses and clothes us.

The point is that transformation isn't something that we can do – only something that Christ can do for us. In the desert of Lent, we walk with Christ, resist temptation and journey on the way to the cross, which is the way to resurrection life. This is why Lent is traditionally the time at which candidates are prepared for baptism on Easter Sunday. Martin Luther captured the meaning of Lenten spirituality when he called on his followers to 'live in your baptism', such that we are continually renewed by the experience of this sacrament. 'Therefore let all Christians regard their Baptism as the daily garment that they are to wear all the time'.[12]

Sacred practice – fasting

The intentional practice of the desert is fasting. This is the central discipline that Jesus modelled in the wilderness, and it's the one that best encapsulates a choice to be stripped back and emptied. The purpose of the fast is not to accumulate 'good works' or to gain any kind of favour in God's eyes – we already have this through the finished work of Christ. Such a focus can only lead to the dead-end of legalism. Rather, the purpose of fasting is 'to establish, maintain, repair, and transform our relationship with God'.[13] We are choosing by the grace of God to step into a disruptive and liminal space for the sake of encounter with God and transformation into his likeness.

In the Old Testament, fasting was associated 'either with particular festivals (such as the Day of Atonement), with particularly intense experiences (as with Moses spending 40 days in the presence of God on Mount Sinai), or with special seasons or feelings'.[14] It does not appear to have been a regular practice. However, by the intertestamental period, fasting seems to have become part of regular devotional activity, and Jesus' own teaching in Matthew 6:1–18 makes clear that fasting is assumed to be a spiritual habit rather than something reserved for special occasions. It would have been the practice of Jesus and his disciples to fast on two days per week, likely from just after breakfast to the time of a light evening meal. Such practice continued for the followers of Jesus, but declined within rabbinical Judaism, which perhaps sought to define itself against the movement of Jesus. Within Greco-Roman culture, the practice of Jesus and his followers would have seemed strange, while at a time of celebration and empire, there was no real need for it. Certain ascetic groups did practise fasting, though when they did this it was a sign of their detachment from the world. The practice of intermittent fasting by Jesus and his followers proclaims something quite different. As Ian Paul writes:

> 'Feast' days celebrated a world made by God and all the good in it; alongside this, 'fast' days signified repentance, mourning and longing for deliverance – just the sort of practice you might adopt if you were awaiting the deliverance of a Messiah and the breaking in of the age to come. Intermittent fasting is just the sort of thing you might continue to practise if you wanted to continue to both affirm the world you lived in, but also to look for an age to come; it is the dietary expression of the 'now and not yet' of the kingdom of God (or, to use a theological term, the 'partially realised eschatology') we find in the New Testament.[15]

This is to say, it is exactly the sort of practice you would expect of people living in the space between and wishing to step into it all the more.

There is great wisdom to be found in the Christian tradition on the practice of fasting. Richard Foster's *Celebration of Discipline* is one of my favourites and here, as elsewhere, he observes that it is wise to 'learn to walk well before we learn to run'.[16] It will be worth building up in fasting – choosing to fast one meal at first, then when we are ready, perhaps two or three, for what would become a 24- or 36-hour fast. Longer fasts of days and weeks might be considered with the right spiritual discernment and physical considerations. However, as things develop, we must stay focused on God, as we can sometimes become overly competitive and find ourselves engaging in ever-more heroic ascetic practices that have lost their inner soul.

Fasting above all else is a cultivation of hunger – a different sort of hunger. It is a stimulation of desire; an expression to God, self and the powers of the world: 'I long for you, God, even more than food (or whatever it is I'm fasting from)'. In dry seasons, it will be more like saying, 'I long to long for you, God. Help me to overcome my lack of longing' (compare Mark 9:24). Its goal, therefore, is positive, not negative, as can be misunderstood. Fasting is an emptying, for the sake of a greater filling. It is a denying of self, for a larger embrace of God. It is a stripping back of what's dead to cultivate all that is fruitful (see John 15:1–2).

I see fasting as a hub practice from which other practices will naturally emerge. It is likely that, in our fasting, we will pair it with prayer and intentionally wait on God to fill our emptiness and soak our dryness. An inward emptying of self will naturally have an outward counterpoint in fasting from money and materialism, to release a greater generosity of giving and service. Isaiah 58 rails against merely an inward practice of fasting that allows grave injustices to continue unabated. It is natural that, in being emptied and hungry, we might have more compassion for those whose ordinary experience of life is only this. Therefore, 'fasting does not stand by itself but must be integrated into a lifestyle emphasising a relationship with God, self and others'.[17]

There will be times when we might share these practices with others; however, it will be important to seek our own time with God as well. The practice of solitude is vital because we can easily use company with others to hide from ourselves. Fasting from people for a short time brings us face-to-face with ourselves. This will be the place where everything unresolved in us rushes to our minds, where the deepest and darkest feelings that we carry present themselves. This is part of the reason so many of us have struggled with the Covid-19 lock-downs – we have been confronted with ourselves with little means of escape. However, desert is the place of warfare and of dying to self. It isn't comfortable, but it does produce in us the fruit of a deeper peace and Christ's resurrection life being birthed more fully in us.

To this end, the story is told about Moses the Black, one of the great desert fathers:

> It happened that Abba Moses was struggling with the temptation of fornication. Unable to stay any longer in the cell, he went and told Abba Isidore. The old man exhorted him to return to his cell. But he refused, saying, 'Abba, I cannot.' Then Abba Isidore took Moses out onto the terrace and said to him, 'Look towards the west.' He looked and saw hordes of demons flying about and making a noise before launching an attack. Then Abba Isidore said to him, 'Look towards the east.' He turned and saw an innumerable multitude of holy angels shining with glory. Abba Isidore said, 'See, these are sent by the Lord to the saints to bring them help, while those in the west fight against them. Those who are with us are more in number than they are.' Then Abba Moses, gave thanks to God, plucked up courage and returned to his cell.

A few lines later in the same collection we read this:

> A brother came to Scetis to visit Abba Moses and asked him for a word. The old man said to him, 'Go, sit in your cell, and your cell will teach you everything.'

What Abba Moses had learned from Abba Isidore he was then able to share with another. His own coming to terms with disruptive and liminal space gave him the ability to prescribe such a wilderness for someone else.

Sacred stories

Historical saints – Antony the Great and William Carey

Antony the Great

From the fourth century AD, an extraordinary phenomenon took place in the deserts of Egypt. The years from about 330 to 340 marked the foundation of the three important monastic centres of Kellia, Nitria and Scetis. As one area became increasingly popular among the monks, and therefore perceived as overcrowded for the taste of hermits, the latter moved to other places to find the necessary solitude. The initial move towards the desert had come partly on account of the persecution of Christians by Decius, causing people to leave the towns and villages of the fertile inhabited regions of the delta around the Nile and to settle in the 'exterior desert'. When the persecution subsided, they plunged deeper into the 'full desert', as it was termed, renouncing their socio-economic world and family life. They were individuals who loved and sought solitude, yet also persons held in community.[18]

According to Athanasius, it was Antony the Great who first settled in the distant territories of the desert to establish ascetical life. His intention was clear: he sought complete solitude and inner tranquillity which he felt was not possible closer to inhabited lands. In his own words: 'He who wishes to live in solitude in the desert is delivered from three conflicts: hearing, speech, and sight; there is only one conflict for him and that is of the heart.'[19] The desert for Antony, therefore, meant stillness; and stillness, wherever achieved, meant desert. The wilderness had a clearly positive connotation for him.

Antony grew up in a well-to-do family. He was only a teenager when his parents both died suddenly, and he rose to the challenge of caring for the home and his younger sister. One Sunday, the gospel lesson was read, 'Go sell all that you have and give to the poor.' The words spoke directly to Antony, and he obeyed them quite literally, making provision for his sister, selling the estate and giving the money to the poor. Such literalism might embarrass us today; however, Antony was railing against a church that was becoming increasingly secularised, and he held out that somehow, in some way, Christians ought to be different.

Antony went into the desert to encounter God, yet this was no time of serenity. He became known as a warrior against demons: fighting spiritual battles both without and within, and wrestling against both what was hostile to human nature and all that was incomplete within human nature. This led to a deep formation of character: 'It was not his physical dimensions that distinguished him from the rest, but the stability of character and the purity of soul. His soul being free of confusion, he held his outer senses also undisturbed, so that from the soul's joy his face was cheerful as well.' This transformation of life became the inspiration for others to imitate. Nor can this be seen as an escape from the world. His time in the desert prepared him for a remarkable ministry of proclamation, apologetics, prophetic challenge and healing.

The wisdom of the desert tradition impacted countless people including Benedict, who organised and adapted it to western conditions, from where it became a major shaping force in European civilisation. This may even have saved western civilisation following the decline of the Roman empire and the advent of the Dark Ages. It is interesting to observe that in the social and economic dislocation of our current time, moves to reclaim the wisdom of the desert and the monastic tradition are gaining popularity.

William Carey

If the desert fathers and mothers sought a more literal experience of the desert, then some 1,500 years later, William Carey knew all too well a metaphorical sense of life in the wilderness.

Carey is often attributed the title 'father of modern missions'. His essay *An Enquiry into the Obligations of Christians to Use Means for the Conversion of the Heathens* led to the founding of the Baptist Missionary

Society. He translated the Bible into Bengali, Oriya, Marathi, Hindi, Assamese and Sanskrit, as well as portions of the Bible into 29 other languages. He made contributions to literature, education, literacy, agriculture, the outlawing of infanticide and the ending of the practice of sati (in which a widow would sacrifice herself by sitting atop her deceased husband's funeral pyre). Carey famously said, 'Expect great things; attempt great things.' It would be easy to look at a 'great' like William Carey and to imagine he was sheltered from the experiences that 'mere mortals' have to go through. Nothing could be further from the truth.

Contrary to Antony, Carey was born into a desperately poor family, as a result of which he obtained a weak education. He was taken on as an apprentice shoemaker, but wasn't good enough to make the grade. He also tried his hand at the running of a school, yet was a failure at this as well. He had an unhappy marriage and his daughter died early, which scarred him for life and caused him to become prematurely bald. Carey was a passionate follower of Jesus, but his attempt at pastoring a small church reduced his chance of ordination as, by common consent, his sermons were too boring for words! One of Carey's great achievements was his translation work; however, at one stage, he lost ten years of such work in a fire at a printing press. Undeterred, Carey went to the spot of the fire and prayed that the work of translation would continue.

Unlike the desert fathers and mothers, William Carey never *chose* the desert, but it seemed that God ordained a desert path to shape Carey for all that Carey would do in his service. Carey was close to death, and knew that one of his supporters wanted to write about his life, so he conveyed his wishes:

> If one should think it worth his while to write my life, I will give you a criterion by which you may judge of its correctness. If he gives me credit for being a plodder, he will describe me justly. Anything beyond this will be too much. I can plod. I can persevere in any definite pursuit. To this I owe everything.

The desert path is not for sprinters. Progress and success will not come quickly in the wilderness. However, a steady plodding through the desolate place with God can see amazing things done for his kingdom.

Contemporary saint

This is the story, in their own words, of a friend who has journeyed, or is still journeying, through the space between.

I didn't want to write anything new as I don't like digging around in those memories, but it does bring me encouragement as well as the pain. I found these cards in my old Bible which were written by me at a very dark and difficult time. There have been plenty more times like these since and even now, but if I remember correctly these words came out of nowhere and gave me some God-given insight into a path longer than the desert one I was wading through at the time. That there would be a way out, and new seasons would be possible, if I hung in there!

I believe that my disappointment, unemployment, depression, illness and loss of direction are all for a greater purpose. Which is to be the bricks which form the foundations, to support the walls, to build the temple, that can house the Holy Spirit from which can flow the purposes of God. I truly believe this, and this alone has kept me going when I could not believe things could have got any worse.

I have been made weak in every way possible in order for me to completely rely on his strength. Any purpose, success or achievement which occurs in my life is a testimony to God working in me and through me. I take no credit or glory, because I will always remember the frailty, helplessness and humanity which I have experienced now.

A song of the wilderness

The wilderness and the dry land shall rejoice,
  the desert shall blossom and burst into song.
They shall see the glory of the Lord,
  the majesty of our God.
Strengthen the weary hands,
  and make firm the feeble knees.
Say to the anxious, 'Be strong, fear not,
  your God is coming with judgement,
  coming with judgement to save you.'
Then shall the eyes of the blind be opened,
  and the ears of the deaf unstopped;
Then shall the lame leap like a hart,
  and the tongue of the dumb sing for joy.
For waters shall break forth in the wilderness,
  and streams in the desert;
The ransomed of the Lord shall return with singing,
  with everlasting joy upon their heads.
Joy and gladness shall be theirs,
  and sorrow and sighing shall flee away.
ISAIAH 35:1, 2B–4A, 4C–6, 10[20]

Questions for reflection

1 What do you 'hunger' and 'thirst' for? Try to be honest with yourself about the mix of desires that you have within you.
2 Which stories or practices from this chapter offer life to you for a desert season?
3 How might you cultivate more of a 'desert space' in your daily, weekly, monthly, termly and annual rhythms?

6

The storm:
when life is shaken

> In fear and amazement they asked one another, 'Who is
> this? He commands even the winds and the water, and they
> obey him.'
> LUKE 8:25

> When you come out of the storm, you won't be the same
> person who walked in. That's what this storm's all about.
> Haruki Murakami[1]

Human emotions – fear and uncertainty

The storm has a long pedigree as a metaphor through which we reflect
upon the difficult times of life.

From *The Tempest* to *King Lear*, Shakespeare used the power of
storms to portray the helpless state of people. In Act I, Scene I of *The
Tempest*, the boatswain reckons that even kings cannot 'command
these elements' of wind and water, and tells Antonio and Sebastian
that they can either 'keep below' or help the sailors. In *King Lear*, the
raging storm on the heath is an apt metaphor for what's going on
inside Lear's mind due to his fury at his daughters' and his own mad-
ness. It also parallels Britain's fall into political chaos as Lear divides
his kingdom.

People react to storms in different ways. Some tingle with excitement about the intensity of strong, roaring winds and powerful, driving rain. They watch the clouds in anticipation and count the seconds between flashes of lightning and rumbles of thunder. Others tremble with anxiety and fear. They hide away under beds or grab hold of others for safety and reassurance. Yet, however the adrenaline moves us, this is all to be something of a spectator to a storm, rather than a proper recipient of its force.

The metaphor of the storm relies on our being exposed to its power, out in the elements as it does its worst. In this way, the image is stark. Storms shake us. They are violent by nature. Times of waiting can feel empty, exile can seem alien, the wilderness bleak; but storms can make us afraid. Their malevolent power hits us head on and there can be nowhere to hide – spiralling winds, deadly lightning and great destruction are left in their wake.

Despite this sobering reality, storms are necessary for sustained life on planet earth. They nourish the soil and cleanse the air. Paradoxical to their fierceness, they are nurturing forces above us and around us. Similarly, the storms of life can be forces for growth in us. They break us open so that we discover, perhaps for the first time, what really lies beneath. This may expose unknown depths of resilience and strength; it may also reveal shadow elements that we wish were not there. Yet the shattering of the storm, in which structures of existence might be brought crashing to the ground, carries with it the opportunity for a rebuilding on firmer foundations. To put it a different way, beyond the storm, we may need to inspect any damage to the boat that is our lives and to consider what debris we are able to salvage. However, there will be new opportunities to sail again upon the waters and even to expand our horizons. Resurrection life always arises from cruciform dying.

During the coronavirus lockdown, as well as before it, thousands of people drew inspiration from the drawings of Charlie Mackesy. One of my favourites is when the boy asks, 'What's the best thing you've learned about storms?' 'That they end,' said the horse.[2] This concurs with the wonderful words of Julian of Norwich, 'All shall be well, and all shall be well and all manner of thing shall be well.' Sometimes we may be able to anticipate this by dancing in the rain before the storm passes; other times we simply need to hold on. To that end, the story is told of an ocean liner that sank off the south-west coast of England, taking many people down with it. A 16-year-old galley boy, who was tossed up along the rugged shore, survived by clinging to a rock all night long. When he was finally rescued, he was asked, 'Didn't you shake as you were clinging all night to that rock?' The boy replied, 'Yes, of course. But the rock never shook once.'[3]

Sacred scriptures

Old Testament – Jonah

The storms of life sometimes seem to come from nowhere. However, on occasion they can be of our own making. When the storm arrives in the Jonah story, it is because he isn't in the place that he should be. Yet there is a powerful reassurance within this story that when life is shaken and heading in all the wrong directions, there is a way in God to 'fall upwards'. In Jonah's story, as keen readers will observe, there are in fact two liminal spaces at work – the storm and also the fish, which functions as a 'pit'. These become for Jonah areas between the settled life that he has known and the new, transformed reality that he will head into. It's these unsettling spaces, out of the usual patterns and routines, comforts and complacencies, that God is able to use to change Jonah. Jonah is able to fall upwards because 'underneath are the everlasting arms' (Deuteronomy 33:27).

Jonah had a call to preach to the great city of Nineveh, an ancient Assyrian city of Upper Mesopotamia, located on the outskirts of Mosul in modern-day northern Iraq. Yet he runs in the opposite direction. He heads *down* to Joppa in order to travel to the far more attractive destination of Tarshish. A violent storm arises, threatening to destroy the ship that he is on and causing great fear even for seasoned sailors on the boat. Yet Jonah has gone *below* deck, where he has laid *down* and *fallen* into a *deep* sleep. When Jonah finally wakes up, he confesses that he is running from the Lord, which terrifies the sailors even more. Jonah is told to get *up* and to call on his God, but the only solution in the end is to cast him *down* into the sea, where he is swallowed by a huge fish.

As the story of Jonah develops, two things occur: Jonah *prays* and Jonah *changes*. The two are not disconnected, as Richard Foster observes:

> To pray is to change. Prayer is the central avenue God uses to transform us. If we are unwilling to change, we will abandon prayer as a noticeable characteristic of our lives.[4]

Research commissioned by the Church of England in 2013 found that only one in seven people insist they would 'never' resort to prayer in the face of problems in their lives, in their friends' lives or in the wider world. So six of every seven people in our society are pray-ers, including teenagers and people in their early 20s, who emerged as less likely to reject prayer than their parents' generation. Storms naturally cause us to pray. Early in the Covid-19 pandemic in April 2020, Jeanet Sinding Bentzen, from the University of Copenhagen, noted a rise in Google searches for 'prayer' across 95 countries and concluded that 'we pray to cope with adversity'. That same instinctive dynamic is at work here with Jonah. In this, Jonah's prayer is *personal*, *honest* and *rich*.

It is *personal* in that the writer says, 'From inside the fish Jonah prayed to the Lord his God' (Jonah 2:1). The Lord is not just God; he is *Jonah's* God. We observed this same dynamic in the story of Jacob at Bethel and in Psalm 63. In prayer in these moments, we claim God for ourselves and allow him to claim us for himself all the more.

Jonah's prayer is *honest* in that he is unafraid to tell the truth about his situation. Jonah says that he called to God from '*deep* in the realm of the dead'; that God 'hurled me into the *depths*', where 'the *deep* surrounded me'; that he had sunk *down* 'to the roots of the mountains', where 'the earth beneath barred me in forever' (Jonah 2:2–3, 5–6). Now we already knew from the narrator where Jonah was, but when we're sinking down it can be hard to tell the truth to ourselves. If we can't tell the truth to ourselves then we're never going to be able to tell the truth to God, even though he already knows it. If we can't tell the truth to God, then where else will we go?

The *richness* of Jonah's prayer comes from the awareness that it contains around 30 references to Old Testament scriptures, most of which are from the Psalms. Jonah can be honest with himself and with God because he has learned a language of prayer from daily meditation upon Israel's sacred songs. If you read the Psalms from start to finish, they are relentlessly honest about what life is really like, far more so still than much of our contemporary language of worship and prayer. Certainly I've found a real liberty in drawing on the wealth and richness of prayers written by others and prayed through the centuries, which draw on scripture and chiefly the book of Psalms.

Jonah prays, and because he opens himself to the Lord in this way, he changes. We can tell this because when Jonah gets his feet on to dry land again, the word of the Lord comes to him a second time and this time he is obedient (Jonah 3:1–3). God changes Jonah in the same way he changes us – through disruption: God uses the times and seasons in which the ordinary and predictable flow of our lives becomes unsettled and disrupted, and he meets us there. (It's important to note that this one episode doesn't bring lasting change to Jonah, so we find him at the end of the story, angry and with a death-wish on himself, on account of God having mercy on Nineveh. Not all change in us is permanent.)

Psalm 29

Two of the psalms we have looked at so far – Psalms 130 and 137 – are psalms of disorientation. The space between is always an experience of being thrown off course, and we need psalms like these to give voice to how we feel and to validate our expressions of lament and complaint before God. This bringing to speech is vital – as Brueggemann argues, disorientation 'may not be fully experienced, embraced, acknowledged, unless and until it is brought to speech'.[5] This is to say, we cannot simply *feel* disoriented in the space between; to move through it in any meaningful way, we must *articulate* our disorientation. With this comes a determination to trust, which was illustrated in Psalm 63. Yet anticipating the next move is also important – the transition to a resolution – and so for this chapter we will look at a psalm of new orientation, Psalm 29. The psalms regularly bear witness to the surprising gift of new life, often when we had assumed that this was no longer possible. This is seldom a return to the old, since this has gone and we also have been changed in the process. Rather, it is the awareness of a new and surprising grace, which cannot be programmed but only received as a gift when it comes.

When God created the heavens and the earth, it was an act of transforming chaos into order. At times, when order seems to give way to chaos, it can feel as though creation is undoing itself. The language of storm and flood is potent for such circumstances (compare Genesis 6—9), where these waters represent chaos. For this reason, when Revelation 21:1 says, 'There was no longer any sea,' it means that in the new creation all chaos is gone forever. In Psalm 29, likely one of the oldest of the psalms, such a future is anticipated in the present as God is celebrated as ruling over the waters and bestowing order and peace again.

The psalm can be seen in three sections: verses 1–2, which constitute a summons to worship; verses 3–9a, that speak of the chaos over which God has been at work; and verses 9b–11, which answer the summons of verses 1–2 as God is enthroned and his people draw strength, blessing and peace from him.

Psalm 29 is a psalm to quell our anxiety when we feel overwhelmed by the storms of life. The whole psalm is cosmic in scale, unlike the personal and intimate psalms of tenderness and pain that we have looked at so far. It will be because of God's cosmic victory that his people are able to enjoy peace and blessing by the end of the psalm. However, the beginning is focused on the 'heavenly beings', God's heavenly council. As in the book of Revelation, there is the assumption that the control centre of the universe is in heaven, and whatever happens there implicitly affects all that takes place on earth. Hence, the worship of heaven – giving glory and strength to God – is something that humans join in with and replicate on earth.

Verses 3–9a present the chaos and cosmic disorientation that God has been at work to overcome. While it may be that there is a specific geographical flow attached to these verses – a rainstorm that sweeps off the Mediterranean Sea (v. 3), heads through Lebanon (vv. 5–6) and on to the southern desert (vv. 7–8) – there is more to it than this. The waters echo those of Genesis 1, 6—9 and speak of global chaos, such that the storm here is an inherent danger to the created order. Any storm in our own lives is similarly a threat to our sense of this order. Yet there is hope, as God is at work to overcome the storm. More specifically, God's voice – named six times in these verses – is able to move decisively to prevent creation unravelling and to put chaos back in its place. It is worth noting that in other psalms, much is made of God's covenant commitment, his love and his faithfulness. Here we are simply confronted with the raw and untamed power of the voice of God, which is over the waters – powerful and majestic, ripping trees apart, striking with flashes of lightning, shaking the desert. The storm may have force, but it is nothing compared to the power of God.

The heavenly beings, summoned to worship in verses 1–2, stand in awe and cry 'glory'. This is something of a delayed response, yet it has taken the evidence of God's power for them to respond as they were commanded. So it may be with us – we may forget God's power until we see it at work again before our eyes. Worshipping in the space between needs an anticipation of God's power at work again in places where that currently does not seem to be the case. This is an act of faith, not of sight.

So it is that God by verse 10 is enthroned over the flood. All is subdued. All is still. What seemed like a force to threaten the whole of the cosmos now sits peacefully beneath his feet. The fruit of victory comes in the blessing which flows from the throne of God. This is the shalom of God, life in all its fullness – wide, vibrant and flourishing – spoken unto creation. It is like the priestly blessing from Numbers 6:22–26; like the angel song of Bethlehem at the beginning of Luke's gospel (Luke 2:14), which proclaimed 'glory' (as in vv. 1–2, 9 here) and then announced 'peace' (v. 11 here) for all the world. It is also like the storm quelled by Jesus the king, on his cross-shaped throne, which enables blessing to flow out to all who open their arms to receive it.

New Testament – Jesus asleep in the boat

Like the sailors on the boat with Jonah, many of Jesus' disciples were highly accomplished at sea. They were seasoned fishermen who would have known the Sea of Galilee as well as anyone. This was their territory – their livelihoods depended on it. Storms and squalls came and went, and they would have known how to cope with them; yet in this episode (Luke 8:22–25), they are taken outside of their ability to manage the situation and beyond their sense of control.

It had all started so well. Jesus had invited them across to the other side of the lake, and all had proved to be plain sailing at first. So much so that Jesus had even been rocked to sleep by the gentle bobbing of the boat upon the water. Quite how things had suddenly got so out of hand was hard to work out. Yet peace and tranquillity were soon overtaken by trouble and threat. A storm descended upon the lake, the boat was swamped and, out of nowhere, the disciples felt in very real danger. Panic set in such that seasoned fishermen were forced to turn to a construction worker for help out at sea. The description recalls the similar situation of Jonah 1:4–6, in which the captain chastises Jonah for sleeping while he and the crew are 'perishing' – it is the same word that is used here when translated, 'We're going to drown' (v. 24).

There is something of a dismissive quality to Jesus' response. What is so far beyond the capacity of the 'experts' to cope with is so comfortably within the bounds of Jesus. There is no fear, no panic, no anxiety in him, simply a commanding rebuke that makes storms subside and peace flood in. In this way, evil powers are brought into submission, and chaos is turned to order in the establishment of God's righteous rule in the world.

Was the miracle of the calming of the storm merely a concession to the disciples and their lack of faith? Did Jesus hope that they could have trusted him to take them through the storm, rather than out of it? How to read his response to the disciples? Exasperation that they should have known better? Or a longing, an aching within him, that they would know this greater way of faith to comprehend that even storms need not unsettle those who are with him? Whichever way it is, there is a chasm to be crossed in the disciples' lived understanding of who Jesus really is: the one who commands even the wind and the waters and they obey him. In this, there is the powerful impression given that to journey with Jesus is never to avoid the storms of life. The storms are not sent by God, but neither does following Jesus give us immunity from them. Sometimes we may be removed from them; more often than not we will be taken through them – for this is how it was for Christ himself. Yet within them, we have a hope that is 'an anchor for the soul, firm and secure' (Hebrews 6:19). It's interesting that an anchor always bears the symbol of the cross within it. This is the source of our hope and the cause of our encouragement: there is something – the death and resurrection of Christ – that goes down below the swirling waters of the storm and holds us, safe and immoveable.

Jesus Christ – Gethsemane (Matthew 14:32–42)

It was in the garden of Gethsemane that Jesus fully and finally embraced his costly vocation to be our anchor. The word 'Gethsemane' means 'oil press' in Hebrew, a fitting name for the spot where the weight of the sin of the world pressed down upon Jesus on the night he was arrested. The garden of Gethsemane on the Mount of Olives was where Jesus prayed in agony, under excruciating pressure. In a storm, there's a force of things happening around us, and being done to us, that we cannot control. Yet Jesus has been there, and he models a way to be faithful to the Father under massive, even overwhelming pressure.

On a trip to the Holy Land a number of years ago, our group visited Jesus's hometown of Nazareth, where we saw an olive press. The press was flanked by an enormous millstone, weighing about 1,100 pounds, which used to crush the olives after the autumn harvest. The olives were placed in a stone pit, and then a donkey was hooked to the millstone to pull the huge stone wheel around in a circle, crushing the olives beneath. The millstone was designed to crush every bit of the olives, the seeds included, in order to turn them into a mash that filled about 15 baskets. This was the crushing stage.

It was followed by the pressing stage, in which the baskets, which had holes in them, were hung on to the long beam of the olive press. The olives underwent three presses, we were told. During the first press, no pressure was put on the baskets and the olive oil simply dripped into a three-foot-deep vat. This first pressing gave the purest oil and was used mainly for lamps, cosmetics and holy anointing. During the second press, a stone weighing about 500 pounds was used to put pressure on the baskets full of olives. Yet there would still remain oil inside the olive mash, so finally as much weight as possible was added to apply even more pressure and to squeeze out the final drops of olive oil.

Three presses – which coincidentally match the three prayers of Jesus in Gethsemane as the weight of the world pressed down on him.

In Mark's gospel, the Gethsemane scene is followed by one of Mark's commonly used sandwich structures, as the trial of Jesus by the Sanhedrin (Mark 14:53–65) is placed between the betrayal of Jesus by Judas (vv. 43–52) and the denial of Jesus by Peter (vv. 66–72). We can all find ourselves caught up in Judas' betrayal and Peter's denial when under pressure. In the Gethsemane scene itself, the disciples are instructed by Jesus to 'stay here and keep watch' (v. 34) and to 'watch and pray' (v. 38); yet three times all they can do is sleep and rest (v. 41). I can recognise that same instinct in myself. When the weight of life bears down, my instinct can be to switch off my connection with all that's around me, even with God. I retreat into my own bubble, where I try to ignore everything. It's a self-preservation device, yet it not only fails to deal with the storm that rages, it also neglects my responsibility to those around me and, most vitally, causes me to lose my connection with Jesus.

In verses 42–52, we see Jesus' response under pressure as he is let down by those around him. Like Jonah, Jesus will fall upward, yet for now his trajectory only sinks down – having come from heaven to earth, he humbles himself even further, being obedient to death, even death on a cross (Philippians 2:8). Jesus is under pressure – 'overwhelmed with sorrow to the point of death,' he says (v. 34), drawing words from Psalms 42—43. In spite of this, he remains in prayer – even as the disciples fall asleep. I find that, under pressure, prayer can sometimes be one of the first things to suffer. Yet without that connection to God, where do we go? It can be easy to have a 'good weather' relationship with God, but not one for a rainy day, let alone a storm. F.B. Meyer said, 'The greatest tragedy of life is not unanswered prayer, but unoffered prayer.' As this incident shows, Jesus, the greater Jonah, had the richness of the Psalms to draw from when he needed to articulate personally and honestly how he felt before the Father. If our language with God is only for the good times, we have a problem. Again, we need to abide deeply in the Psalms.

I've found the pattern of Jesus' prayer in Gethsemane, in verse 36, incredibly helpful in my own praying under pressure. There are four parts to it:

1 *Abba, Father* – Jesus affirms his belief in God as all-good and all-loving.
2 *Everything is possible for you* – Jesus affirms his belief in God as all-powerful and able to do all things.

3 *Take this cup from me* – Jesus lays out his specific request in prayer.
4 *Yet not what I will, but what you will* – Jesus submits himself to the
Father's will.

It's amazing to note that Jesus' prayer here was *not* answered. He prayed to be delivered from the cross, and he wasn't. We all struggle with unanswered prayer; in the same way here, Jesus, the Son of God, has to live with unanswered prayer. Yet crucially, he submits. He can submit because he is able to affirm both the goodness and the power of God and to keep an honest channel open to God through which he can ask him anything. Jesus is faithful unto death, even death upon a cross.

In late 2010/early 2011, my dad had a number of seizures. These were initially put down to epilepsy and treated with medication. For just short of a year, this seemed to be keeping things under control. However, further seizures in February/March 2012 showed that deeper investigation was required. A diagnosis was given of a grade-4, fast-growing glioblastoma, a malignant tumour. Surgery was undertaken to remove as much as possible, followed by radiotherapy and chemotherapy. Initially the tumour was contained, but the treatment brought many side effects, and eventually chemotherapy had to be cut short. On 7 November 2012, Dad had a final seizure from which he never woke up. He died four days later on Remembrance Day.

Throughout this time, I tried to balance my own sense of grief with a desire to be strong for my mum and the rest of the family. I thought I was holding it together, but my body was telling me differently. I suddenly found I couldn't run without having to take an inhaler with me. My eczema returned, for the first time in 25 years or so. I was training to be a vicar, and I had all sorts of questions about God and life and faith that tumbled out of this. How was I to make sense of the injustice of the whole thing? Dad had just reached retirement age – he had worked hard, earned the chance to spend time with his family, his grandchildren especially, and all of that had suddenly evaporated.

Throughout Dad's illness, I came to find in the prayer of Jesus in Gethsemane a model for how I could pray in the storm:

1 *Abba, Father* – I tried to hold on to a belief in God as compassionate and good in spite of all that was happening. A Matt Redman song, 'You Never Let Go', based on Psalm 23 and affirming God as loving, was really important for me.
2 *Everything is possible for you* – I tried to anchor myself in a knowledge of God as all-powerful. Another song called 'Sovereign Over Us', which speaks of God's plan being still to prosper us, helped to keep hold of a vision of God as sovereign and all-powerful.
3 *Take this cup from me* – Right to the end, I was praying that my dad would be healed, as I laid out this prayer before God.
4 *Yet not what I will, but what you will* – I found this incredibly hard to do, but I kept trying to pray it, even though I often felt that my will was better. Submitting ourselves to God's will in the storm is agonising. To echo this difficult prayer in our own lives, we have to trust that God's perspective is greater and his plans are better than our own. To truly pray, 'Your will be done,' we need to surrender the place of highest authority in our lives – no easy feat.

In Gethsemane, Jesus offers a model for honest, broken, vulnerable prayer under excruciating pressure in the midst of the storm. Psalm 23 describes the darkest of seasons as opportunities for God to anoint us with oil and for our cup to spill over. Within the storm, weighed down, there is something precious that can flow out. In my experience, however, this does take time.

Sacred time – Good Friday

On Good Friday, we gaze upon the crucified Jesus. Jesus' primary instinct in those moments before his death was to pray – crying out personally to his Father, telling the truth of his sense of being abandoned by God, and drawing on the wealth and richness of the Psalms, in which he was steeped. He is the one who, when the Pharisees asked him for a sign to prove who he was, would speak only 'the sign of the prophet Jonah'. Just as Jonah spent 'three days and three nights in the belly of a huge fish', so Jesus, the one who is 'greater than Jonah', would spend 'three days and three nights in the heart of the earth' (Matthew 12:38–42).

The cross of Jesus Christ brings us to the centre of our faith, and each of the metaphors that we have been exploring provides a perspective upon it. The death of Jesus Christ unleashes the agony of divine delay, as days of waiting follow; the cross is the wilderness in which Jesus is stripped naked for all to see; it is the alien place to which he is exiled; and his tomb will be the pit of deep darkness in which he is abandoned. Using the metaphor of this chapter, the cross is the ultimate storm, unleashed with full force and fury upon Jesus.

On Good Friday, the unfettered power of the tsunami of human sin and cosmic chaos was let loose. As lightning struck, the cross acted as a kind of conductor with its focal point the body of Jesus Christ. A lightning conductor is a metal rod, mounted on a structure and intended to protect the structure from the strike. If lightning hits the structure, it will preferentially strike the rod and be 'conducted' to ground through a wire, instead of passing through the structure where it could start a fire or cause electrocution. In this way, the storm struck and did its worst to Jesus, so that its fury might not be unleashed upon us. The lightning struck and hit the rod not the structure, protecting us all from its impact.

As the prophet Isaiah phrased it so beautifully:

Surely he took up our pain
  and bore our suffering,
yet we considered him punished by God,
  stricken by him, and afflicted.
But he was pierced for our transgressions,
  he was crushed for our iniquities;
the punishment that brought us peace was on him,

> *and by his wounds we are healed.*
> *We all, like sheep, have gone astray,*
> * each of us has turned to our own way;*
> *and the Lord has laid on him*
> * the iniquity of us all.*
> ISAIAH 53:4–6

These verses challenge us. They express a reality to which we must respond, and which John Stott has framed so clearly: 'Before we can begin to see the cross as something done for us (leading to faith and worship), we have to see it as something done by us (leading us to repentance).'[6] Indeed, 'only the person who is prepared to own their share in the guilt of the cross,' wrote Canon Peter Green, 'may claim their share in its grace.'[7] Good Friday confronts us that we might come to a place where we can say that it was *my* sin that put Jesus on the cross. We may or may not be complicit in the storms that we experience in the disruptive seasons of our lives; however, we are all complicit in the storm that did its worst to Jesus Christ, and a full acknowledgement of this is the only way through our own storms. There is an inherent tension in Good Friday, as revealed in its name, which also captures the very tension inherent in the space between. How can the day be said to be 'good', for it was a day of horror as Jesus suffered pain and torture that he did not deserve? And yet in the way that his death would cause the death of all death, it was so very 'good'.

Churches across the world mark Good Friday in a number of different ways, three of which are perhaps the most common.[8] First, and least familiar to myself, is the Catholic tradition of the Veneration of the Cross. Clergy and congregation approach a cross or crucifix one by one and offer a gesture of respect to all that it represents. This gesture usually includes kneeling or bowing before the cross and then kissing it. Second, the tradition of the Stations of the Cross marks a way of following the journey of Jesus to Golgotha through nine scenes drawn from the gospel accounts and five from popular tradition.[9] This captures something of the experience of pilgrimage that can be powerful in our liminal seasons of life. Third, the Three Hours at the Cross focuses on the last sayings of Jesus as a way of connecting with the suffering that Jesus endured on the cross.[10] This links with the disciplines of fasting and silence covered elsewhere in this book.

Sacred practice – complaint

Lament [or complaint/protest] is the ravaged heart's cry to the source of her being, the inconsolable ranting that reaches out to demand an end to suffering, the fierce force of living in the face of death that turns towards God in irresolute hope.[11]

The complaint psalm is a painful expression of what it means to move into a time of dislocation, whether for an individual[12] or for the community.[13] It is a reluctant embrace of the new situation which acknowledges the chaos and lack of coherence in the world all around. It might be personal and intimate, or communal and public. In both cases it expresses a sense of an 'end of the world' experience. Nonetheless, what is distinctive in this move is the conviction that this experience of disorientation has everything to do with God and therefore must be addressed to God. For this reason, over a third of the Psalms are complaint, lament or protest psalms – as many as 67 out of 150. They should not be judged as acts betraying faith but rather as acts of bold and profound faith, for at least two reasons. First, they display the honesty to say things as they really are, to represent the world as it is and not as we might wish, or might pretend, it to be. Second, they display a boldness that views these thoughts as thoroughly appropriate to express to God. God does not seek a redacted version of our sentiments – he wishes to hear them all, unfiltered. As Brueggemann writes:

Nothing is out of bounds, nothing precluded or inappropriate. Everything properly belongs in this conversation of the heart. To withhold parts of life from that conversation is in fact to withhold part of life from the sovereignty of God. Thus the Psalms make the important connection: everything must be brought to speech, and everything brought to speech must be addressed to God, who is the final reference for all of life.[14]

We do not worship merely a 'good-time God', but one who is with us in our pain and suffering. Moreover, this can only really be meaningful if we understand this God to be one 'of suffering, and familiar with pain' (see Isaiah 53:3). Therefore, our entire conception of God needs to come under the microscope as part of our journey through the space between. Dietrich Bonhoeffer implores us to see the distinction between the God of Christianity and merely a religious god:

> This is the decisive difference between Christianity and all religions. Man's religiosity makes him look in his distress to the power of God in the world; he uses God as a deus ex machina. The Bible, however, directs us to the powerlessness and suffering of God; only a suffering God can help. To this extent we may say that the process we have described by which the world came of age was an abandonment of the false conception of God, and a clearing of the decks for the God of the Bible, who conquers power and space in the world by his weakness.[15]

The Psalms enable us to clear the decks for the God of the Bible. They allow us to worship and pray to God as God is, not as the slot machine with whom we might sometimes wish to transact. They facilitate genuine relationship to take place in which we are prepared to share and express all that we are, not merely the selected and edited highlights. They also enable us to make sense of our experiences by giving language to them – the language of those who, while unfamiliar with the specifics of our circumstances, have experienced the same emotions as ourselves. When we complain to God, our problems don't get magically fixed, but our lives are being spiritually formed.

Westermann divides the basic structure of complaint psalms into two halves: *plea* (the complaint that God should correct) and *praise* (the response to a change of situation). The *plea* half has five basic elements to it:

1 *Address to God* – personal and intimate.
2 *Complaint* – the nature of the problem is set out.
3 *Petition* – the request is made.
4 *Motivation* – reasons are given as to why God should act, either based on the actions of the person or the nature of God.
5 *Imprecation* – unguarded language which strays into resentment and revenge, but is not edited out.

The *praise* half has three elements:

1 *Assurance of being heard* – the shift from no longer feeling God as distant, to now being sure that he has heard our plea.
2 *Payment of vows* – the acting on any promises that were made in the motivation section above if God acted.
3 *Doxology and praise* – God is honoured as good, faithful, generous and saving.

There are a number of ways to explain the surprising shift between *plea* and *praise* in these psalms of complaint. Some think that the praise section was a later addition, others that the expression of complaint now facilitates an expression of praise, as things that needed to be said have been said. The most widespread view is that of the theologian Joachim Begrich, who believes that an authorised speaker would respond to the plea in a standard 'deliverance oracle' – such as we find in Jeremiah 30:10–11, Isaiah 41:8–13 and Isaiah 43:1–7. The theory goes that these originally stood in the space between the two elements of the psalm, and have now become independent units within scripture. At their core, such oracles proclaim that the person in the situation should not be afraid because God is present and able to help and intervene. We all know the power of being heard, the comfort of a presence with us and the knowledge that someone in authority can act on our behalf. This is what we long for from God in the space between.

It can be a powerful step for us to express our own laments or complaints to God. As we explored earlier, our own prayers can sometimes be far too polite for moments like this, while under pressure we can even drop the connection altogether. John Swinton in *Raging with Compassion* suggests a structure for us, derived from the layout of the psalms of complaint above.[16]

1 *Address God* – We call on God by name, using any names or titles that speak to us or which express qualities of God that we want to call upon. We might use many names.
2 *Complain* – We make this detailed: what has happened? Who is hurting and why? Whose fault, if anyone's, is it? We express everything to God, and try to leave nothing held back.
3 *Express trust in our relationship with God* – This might be a single sentence. For example, Lamentations 3:24: 'I say to myself, "The Lord is my portion; therefore I will wait for him"', or words from Psalm 63 above.
4 *Appeal/petition* – This is a cry that God would intervene and is usually accompanied by the reason for needing the intervention. Several appeals might be made.
5 *Optional: Vow your praise* – Terrible things have happened, and yet we still commit to praise God. This last step is optional because the complaint must be true to where we are in the moment. Praise may come later, perhaps after an assurance of deliverance is received. The important thing is that the complaint is authentic.

Sacred stories

Historical saints – John Newton and Horatio Spafford

John Newton
Storms can be deeply transformative moments in our lives. Sometimes they can scare us into new possibilities.

John Newton was born in 1725 in London. His mother was a godly woman who taught him to pray as a child, but she died when he was only seven years old. He had just two years at school before at the age of eleven his father, who was a sea captain, took him to sea for the first time. In 1743 Newton was on his way to a position as a slave master on a plantation in Jamaica when he was pressed into naval service. He became a midshipman, but after demotion for trying to desert, he requested an exchange to a slave ship bound for West Africa. Eventually he reached the coast of Sierra Leone, where he became the servant of an abusive slave trader.

Newton was rescued from this servitude by a friend of his father, who was a ship's captain as well. Newton lit a fire of driftwood on the shore to attract the attention of any passing ship. In the providence of God, this friend of his father, who was searching for him, sent a longboat ashore to investigate, and John was rescued. He was on this ship returning across the Atlantic when on 10 March 1748 it encountered a great storm that was threatening to engulf it. 'That 10th of March', says Newton, 'is a day much to be remembered by me; and I have never allowed it to pass unnoticed since the year 1748. For on that day the Lord came from on high and delivered me out of deep waters.' Newton had been reading Thomas à Kempis's *The Imitation of Christ* and was struck by a line about the 'uncertain continuance of life'.

The storm was terrible. When the ship plunged down into the trough of the sea, few on board expected it to come up again. The hold was rapidly filling with water. As Newton hurried to his place at the pumps he said to the captain, 'If this will not do, the Lord have mercy upon us!' His own words startled him. 'Mercy!' he said to himself in astonishment, 'Mercy! Mercy! What mercy can there be for me? This was the first desire I had breathed for mercy for many years!' About six in the evening the hold was free from water, and then came a gleam of hope. 'I thought I saw the hand of God displayed in our favour. I began to pray. I could not utter the prayer of faith. I could not draw near to a reconciled God and call him Father. My prayer for mercy was like the cry of the ravens, which yet the Lord does not disdain to hear.'

This experience began his conversion to evangelical Christianity. He converted during the storm, though he admitted later, 'I cannot consider myself to have been a believer, in the full sense of the word.' Later, while aboard a slave vessel bound for the West Indies, he became ill with a violent fever and asked for God's mercy – another storm-like experience that Newton claimed was a turning point in his life. Though Newton continued in his profession of sailing and slave-trading for a time, his life was slowly transformed. He began a disciplined schedule of Bible study, prayer and Christian reading, and tried to be a Christian example to the sailors under his command. Philip Doddridge's *The Rise and Progress of Religion in the Soul* provided much spiritual comfort, while a fellow Christian captain whom he met off the coast of Africa guided Newton further in his Christian faith. Newton wrote:

> It is certain that I am not what I ought to be. But, blessed be God, I am not what I once was. God has mercifully brought me up out of the deep miry clay and set my feet upon the Rock, Christ Jesus. He has saved my soul. And now it is my heart's desire to extol and honour his matchless, free, sovereign and distinguishing grace, because 'By the grace of God I am what I am' [1 Corinthians 15:10]. It is my heart's great joy to ascribe my salvation entirely to the grace of God.[17]

Newton left slave-trading and took the job of tide surveyor at Liverpool, but he began to sense a call to ordained ministry. His mother's prayers for her son were answered when, in 1764, at the age of 39, John Newton began 43 years of preaching the gospel of Christ. John and his beloved wife Mary moved to the little market town of Olney. He spent his mornings in Bible study and his afternoons visiting his parishioners. There were regular Sunday morning and afternoon services, as well as meetings for children and young people. There was also a Tuesday evening prayer meeting which was always well attended.

For the Sunday evening services, Newton often composed a hymn that developed the lessons and scripture for the evening. In 1779, 280 of these were collected and combined with 68 hymns by Newton's friend and parishioner, William Cowper, and published as the Olney Hymns. The most famous of all the Olney Hymns, 'Faith's Review and Expectation', grew out of David's exclamation in 1 Chronicles 17:16–17. We know it today as 'Amazing Grace'. Several other Olney hymns by Newton continue in use today, including 'How Sweet the Name of Jesus Sounds' and 'Glorious Things of Thee are Spoken'.

In 1779 Newton left Olney to become rector of St Mary Woolnoth in London. His ministry encompassed not only the London poor and the merchant class but also the wealthy and influential. William Wilberforce, a member of Parliament and a prime mover in the abolition of slavery, was strongly influenced by John Newton's life and preaching, while missionaries William Carey and Henry Martyn also gained strength from his counsel. Newton's pamphlet *Thoughts Upon the African Slave Trade*, which was based on his own experiences as a slave trader, was very important in securing the British abolition of slavery.

Newton lived to be 82 years old and continued to preach and have an active ministry until beset by fading health in the final two or three years of his life. Even then, Newton never ceased to be amazed by God's grace and told his friends, 'My memory is nearly gone; but I remember two things: that I am a great sinner, and that Christ is a great Saviour.'

Horatio Spafford

For John Newton, a storm threw him upon God's mercy in a new way. For Horatio Spafford, the storms he encountered served to confirm the grace of God that was already at work in him.

Spafford was a senior partner in a thriving law firm and a devout Presbyterian church elder. He lived a comfortable life with his wife, Anna, and their four young daughters and a son in Chicago. At their home in a north-side suburb of Chicago, the Spaffords hosted and sometimes financially supported many guests. Horatio had been active in the abolitionist crusade, and their cottage was a meeting place for activists in the reform movements of the time, such as

Frances E. Willard, president of the Woman's Christian Temperance Union, and for evangelical leaders, such as Dwight L. Moody, who ignited a religious revival in America and Europe. However, their comfort was soon to be interrupted. In 1871, his son died of scarlet fever, aged four. Later that year, a great fire broke out and devastated the entire city. Spafford had invested heavily in real estate along Lake Michigan's shoreline, and he lost everything overnight.

Two years later, the family decided to take a holiday with friends in Europe, to benefit Anna's health, and to assist Moody and his musician Ira Sankey in one of their campaigns in Great Britain. At the last moment, Horatio was detained by business, and Anna and the girls went on ahead, sailing on the ocean liner *S.S. Ville du Havre*. On 21 November 1873, the liner was hit by a British vessel and sank within minutes. Anna was picked up unconscious on a floating spar, but the four children had already drowned. A fellow survivor of the collision, Pastor Weiss, recalled Anna saying, 'God gave me four daughters. Now they have been taken from me. Someday I will understand why.' Nine days after the shipwreck, Anna landed in Cardiff, Wales, and cabled Horatio: 'Saved alone. What shall I do?'

After receiving Anna's telegram, Horatio immediately left Chicago to bring his wife home. On the Atlantic crossing, the captain of his ship called Horatio to his cabin to tell him that they were passing over the spot at which his four daughters had perished. He wrote to Rachel, his wife's half-sister, 'On Thursday last we passed over the spot where [the ship] went down, in mid-ocean, the waters three miles deep. But I do not think of our dear ones there. They are safe, folded, the dear lambs.'

Horatio wrote a hymn as he passed over their watery grave, which still brings peace and assurance to many today:

When peace like a river attendeth my way,
when sorrows like sea billows roll;
whatever my lot, thou hast taught me to say,
'It is well, it is well with my soul.'

It is well with my soul;
It is well, it is well with my soul.

Such lyrics should not be understood as a way of avoiding pain, and pretending that everything is okay when it is not. They do not preclude a voicing of grief, anguish and complaint to God. However, within this process, by the grace of God, we are able to come to a place of submission and surrender where we can say, 'Not my will, but yours be done' and can sing, 'It is well with my soul.'

Contemporary saint

This is the story, in their own words, of a friend who has journeyed, or is still journeying, through the space between.

In the week before our son was born, I read a poem by Norah Hanson. She described the arrival of a child as a force against which there is no defence. I had no connection with her words. In fact, I disliked the poem and the insinuation that the gift of a new child could usher in a storm. But, in time, the raw honesty of Hanson's words in 'Grafters' would become an anchor in an otherwise wordless, disorienting experience.

There was a calm before. A clarity. I have rarely experienced a season of such contentment as I did in pregnancy. In many ways, I love living life on a threshold, on the edge of something new, when everything is vision, possibility and alive with potential. I was so confident approaching motherhood. So unafraid. So relaxed.

So, I did not see it coming – the storm. There was no time to anticipate or brace.

There was a turning point about 24 hours into labour. The peaceful surroundings of my longed-for natural homebirth were traded for a traumatic ambulance ride and an emergency C-section. I had felt in control and focused; I became inconsolable and overwhelmed. Extreme emotions were traded.

Initially I thought the storm was short-lived – a whirlwind of fear uprooting us only momentarily. Our son was born healthy; I was healthy. 'Surely that's all that matters,' I was told repeatedly. And certainly in the initial hours, days, even weeks of his little life, the dust seemed to settle. What kicked it up again? I don't know. Perhaps I buried my head in the sand for a while, refusing to acknowledge the complexity of my emotions.

It was blizzard-like. Steady and persistent. The sleeplessness. The constant crying. The loneliness. The steady drain on all my resources. I berated myself, refusing to acknowledge that I was struggling to cope. It was unexpected, and I found myself hard to recognise. My joy was thin. My creativity sapped. I feared going out and about, no longer the extrovert.

There were times when the clouds parted. Peace. Stillness. Togetherness relished as a little family of three. But then things would cloud up again, my vision would blur (literally – I've never cried so much) and the only words I could find to accurately describe my emotions seemed extreme and out of place. How could I own them? How could this be grief when I had a beautiful child in my arms? I refused to give in and fought to control a storm I had no control over.

Could I have taken shelter? 'The Lord is my rock… in whom I take refuge' (Psalm 18:2). Was the worst part of the storm that I couldn't find my rock to shelter behind? Where was Jesus? Asleep in the boat as I battled with the waves? In the storm, my theology didn't help me. I knew he was there, present through it all. How often I had told others about his gentle, loving, transformative silence? But the peace of his silence and the power of his words did not reach me through the crying and exhaustion. I did not feel his touch. The purpose of God's absence was lost on me.

In time, the storm subsided. But the landscape has changed. I have changed. My view has changed. So much has been pulled down that sometimes it seems frighteningly bare. All the structures that once held things in place are gone, but it feels as though I can see for miles now. I let go of a lot of baggage in the storm. I feel raw and bare before God again. And he occupies the wide-open space before me.

A prayer in the storm

> *God of the Universe, at the dawn of creation, your Spirit breathed on the waters, making them the wellspring of all holiness. You created the oceans and rivers, and all that dwell within them, and at your word the wind and the waves were born.*
>
> *The seasons follow your plan, and the tides rise and fall on your command. In both calm and storm, you are with us.*
>
> *On the Sea of Galilee, even when the disciples began to fear, Jesus showed that he was Lord over the waters by rebuking the storms, so that all would know that even the wind and the waves obey him.*
>
> *Creator God, we ask you to calm the wind and the waves of the approaching hurricane, and spare those in its path from harm. Help those who are in its way to reach safety. Open our hearts in generosity to all who need help in the coming days.*
>
> *In all things and in all times, help us to remember that even when life seems dark and stormy, you are in the boat with us, guiding us to safety. Amen.*

James Martin, S.J.[18]

Questions for reflection

1 Where does anxiety, fear, and stress play a part in your life? What are the triggers and how do you normally cope?
2 What resources from the chapter give you strength for the storm?
3 Write a prayer of complaint to God – about something in your life, the life of someone near to you or something in the world at present.

7

The pit:
when life sinks to the bottom

**He lifted me out of the slimy pit, out of the mud and mire;
he set my feet on a rock and gave me a firm place to stand.**
PSALM 40:2

**We must tell people what we have learned here. We must tell
them that there is no pit so deep that he is not deeper still.**
Betsie ten Boom about Ravensbrück concentration camp[1]

Human emotions – darkness and despair

When life sinks down, everything goes dark and we find ourselves in
the pit. We feel as though we're at the bottom. There's nowhere further
down that we can go and there doesn't appear to be any way out.
Whether we were thrown in, slipped in or jumped in, there can be an
overriding sense of despair and hopelessness. Life feels inescapably
bleak in the pit.

In the Old Testament, the pit was a large hole in the ground. It might
be used to catch wild animals (Ezekiel 19:1–8) or to collect water for
drinking, as in a cistern (Deuteronomy 6:11). Sometimes pits were used
as dungeons or prisons (Genesis 37:24; Exodus 12:29; Jeremiah 38:6).
Each of these uses provides a lens for what it can feel like for us in
the pit. It can seem as though we've lost something of our humanity
through what's brought us here. The place for sustaining life is bone

dry and now we're trapped inside it. The pit was commonly used as a metaphor for Sheol (Psalm 16:10; Psalm 30:9). Everyone dies, therefore no one can avoid the pit (Psalm 49:9), which captures its futility. It is a place of destruction (Isaiah 38:17), dark and deep, where the dead are without strength, forsaken by the living and forgotten by God (Psalm 88:3–6). There is no thanksgiving, praise or hope here (Psalm 38:1–8). The expectation of resurrection appeared late on Israel's horizon and so expressions of the pit are naturally bleak and negative.

In the New Testament, the pit can still be a hole that an animal might fall into (Luke 14:5) and it is still used for the place of the dead (Romans 10:7). However, its uses became more cosmic, dark and severe, such that it is the abode of demons (Luke 8:31). In the book of Revelation, it is taken into the imagination of the writer to become an abyss – a deep or seemingly bottomless chasm under the earth with a shaft that connects it to the surface, and smoke that comes out of the shaft like a furnace (Revelation 9:1–2, 11). It is the place from which the beast will emerge. It is where Satan will be bound for a thousand years after which he will be cast into a lake of fire. There's a sense here that our own personal darkness is part of a much deeper, cosmic darkness that pervades the world.

My own experience of the pit came after the death of my dad. Taking place at the time of my training to be a vicar, it felt that I should have had the learning to equip me to deal with this sort of event, although none of us ever do. When it hit me, I sank right down and didn't know at all where I was. In truth, all my instincts were to avoid even an admission of my being in the pit. A month after my dad's death, I was at a college Christmas dinner, but I simply couldn't handle the incongruence of the mood around me with what had happened only weeks before. I had thought that by going I might receive a helpful distraction, yet the noise around me, and the noise in my head, were simply unbearable. I just wanted to numb everything, so I kept on drinking. I was violently sick on the way home. When I came around the next day, I realised I was in a place that I'd never been in before. It felt frighteningly bleak.

There's something of the short, sharp shaking of the storm that is genuinely scary, yet the pit is different. The horror of the pit comes, but then it endures – what makes it frightening is that you don't know when, or even if, you will make it out. Yet, even here there is hope. This is why Aleksandr Solzhenitsyn – who spent eight years in prisons and labour camps for his criticism of Joseph Stalin, then three more in enforced exile – was able to say, 'sometimes to the astonishment of those around me, "Bless you, prison!… Bless you, prison, for having been in my life." For there, lying upon the rotting prison straw, I came to realize that the object of life is not prosperity as we are made to believe, but the maturity of the human soul.'[2] For myself, I recognise the pit to be the place in which I have done the deepest wrestling regarding who I am, what has happened to me, and who I am called to become.

Sacred scriptures

Old Testament – Job

The story of Job is often turned to by those seeking to make sense of life at the bottom. It is the third of the Bible's wisdom books. The first, the book of Proverbs, asserts that the world is wise and just, and that people get what they deserve. The second, the book of Ecclesiastes, argues that this isn't always the case, and that the world is often quite unpredictable and difficult to comprehend. The book of Job focuses the debate more on God and considers whether he is, in fact, just, given the way that the world is. It's written by an anonymous author and is set in an obscure land, at an unknown time, with a main character who isn't an Israelite. Clearly questions of history and context are not at the forefront here, as we are invited to take a wider view of the problems being raised.

Job is presented as a blameless, upright man, who fears the Lord and shuns evil. The scene shifts to God's 'staff team' in the heavenly command centre and to a shadowy figure, the 'satan' – or accuser – who makes a play. This character questions the way in which God is running the show and argues that Job is simply gaming the system. Job is only good, the argument runs, because he is blessed with abundance: take this away and you will see the true Job! God goes along with this, although the reasons for this are never explored in the story. As Job begins to lose everything, his pious expressions of faith give way to more honest articulations of how he really feels as he quickly curses the day on which he was born. Job has been set off on an emotional roller coaster, on which he is up, down and all over the place. In this, he is not helped at all by those around him – his wife and four 'friends'.

The difficulty for all involved in the story is the presuppositions they each bring to the conundrum of suffering and pain. We all bring presumptions of our own to such great questions of life and faith. Job's three initial friends violate the situation by charging in with their already-formed conclusion that, because God is just and the world is run according to justice, Job must have done something to deserve his suffering. They speculate, unhelpfully, on the sins he must have committed. We might think that such simplistic formulations would have had their day, yet it is interesting to observe how they still circulate when life sinks to the bottom. The formulation can also play in our own heads when we ourselves hit the pit, as the 'accuser' continues to do his shadowy work.

Yet Job knows that something isn't right in this logical sequence. (We as the reader know it isn't correct, as the narrator has already told us that Job is innocent.) Job is clear that his suffering cannot be divine justice, and he is left with only two possible conclusions: either God doesn't run the world according to divine justice or, even more shockingly, God himself isn't just. (Job's wife offers him a third alternative – curse God and die! – though this is given short shrift.) Job's emotional roller coaster, stemming from all that he is unable to reconcile, leads to some outbursts against God – including that God is a bully and even the orchestrator of all injustice. Yet in this, Job still longs to believe and is terrified of the implications of what he is saying.

A fourth friend, Elihu, enters the scene and offers a more nuanced suggestion – that Job's suffering might have the dual purpose of warning him to avoid future sin and building his character. There are a lot of Elihus around today, so keen to resolve the excruciating tension of suffering and to explain to those in pain why God allowed this or that to take place. Job doesn't even respond to Elihu, as he soon gives up on his friends and takes up his case directly with God.

Out of the storm cloud, God responds personally to Job. God, like a street poet, gives Job something of a virtual tour of the universe, taking in its origins and design.

> *Where were you when I laid the earth's foundation?*
>   *Tell me, if you understand.*
> JOB 38:4

> *What is the way to the abode of light?*
>   *And where does darkness reside?*
> *Can you take them to their places?*
>   *Do you know the paths to their dwellings?*
> JOB 38:19–20

> *Do you know when the mountain goats give birth?*
>   *Do you watch when the doe bears her fawn?*
> JOB 39:1

For two entire chapters, the rhetorical questions are piled one upon another, as Job is alerted to intricate, cosmic details he could never have conceived of. In this, there is a deconstruction of all of Job's assumptions. The universe is vast and complex and, while God has his eyes on this, Job has only a limited view from which he cannot properly judge. God has a vastly bigger perspective, dynamically interacting in this world of complexity, which is his wisdom to do. Job comes to recognise that he has nothing to say. Mysteriously, the behemoth and the leviathan are celebrated by God – part of his good world, yet remaining symbols of disorder and danger in it. No explanation is given for the extreme and complex world that God has created and within which Job lives. Job retracts what he has said, and, while his friends are judged to have spoken wrongly, Job is said to have spoken rightly – clearly not in everything that he has said, but in his wrestling directly with God and his honesty with him. In the end, Job receives back double for what he has lost, not as a reward but as a generous gift.

It is important to realise that the book of Job does not unlock the puzzle of why bad things happen to good people. The search for reasons for our suffering and the suffering of others – any seeking of purposes and goals to ascribe to them – is all exposed as something we are not positioned to do. It merely adds layers of anguish on to the existing presence of pain. Job only really begins to see sense when he falls silent, humbles himself and is able to live in peace and the fear of the Lord, without explanation. That being said, the offering of his pain and grief to God, in spite of the specifics that are vented, is clearly affirmed. The world has order and beauty, but it is also wild and dangerous – within this, there is simply the invitation to trust in God's wisdom within it.

There is also the hope that, even though causes are not understood and God may feel absent, nonetheless, formational good will emerge:

But if I go to the east, he is not there;
  if I go to the west, I do not find him.
When he is at work in the north, I do not see him;
  when he turns to the south, I catch no glimpse of him.
But he knows the way that I take;
  when he has tested me, I will come forth as gold.
JOB 23:8–10

Psalm 88

Psalm 88 is a psalm for those in despair. Strikingly, Walter Brueggemann writes that the psalm 'is an embarrassment to conventional faith'.[3] Psalm 88 is the most extreme of the complaint psalms; however, it is the most extraordinary gift to the person living in desperate times to which conventional faith is unable to give voice. The psalm is held together by the structure of a threefold 'cry' of verses 1–2, 9b and 13. Throughout scripture, God is known as the one who always hears the cry of his people. However, here that cry is not being apprehended.

The first cries of verses 1–2 begin in familiar fashion. There is an intimate appeal to God as the one who is able to turn the situation around. Yet divine silence will mean that this is the only petition made in the entire psalm. From verses 3–9, the words become ever more descriptive and ever more intense. The experience of the psalmist is laid out in powerful detail – full of trouble and feeling close to death. This is the experience of the pit: a sense of weakness and powerlessness, as though life has come to its end. Yet the psalmist is not prepared to leave things here. Instead, the horror of being remembered no more by God and cut off from his care leads to ever bolder and more strident accusations. The words of verses 6–9a might have come from the mouth of Job – God, *you* have put me here, *your* wrath lies upon me, *you* have overwhelmed me, *you* have taken from me, *you* have made me this way. Unlike in the book of Job, there is no effort to understand things theologically in this psalm, simply to express the psalmist's raw emotion.

After the second cry of verse 9b, verses 10–12 contain a series of six rhetorical questions. Just as God answered Job in the whirlwind with a series of rhetorical questions – to which the anticipated answer was in the negative – so here the psalmist answers the silence of God in the same way. The supposed character of God – his wonders, praise, love, faithfulness, wonders again and righteous deeds – are all contrasted with the lived reality of the psalmist in the place of death, dead spirits, the grave, destruction, darkness and oblivion. The gap is exposed between who God says he is and where the psalmist is currently located. The end feels very near, and still there is only silence from God.

The third and final cry comes in verse 13. There are similarities with the first section, in that the experience of the psalmist is again described in painful detail – full as it is of a lifetime of suffering and near-death experience, of terror and despair. Yet the accusation of culpability is laid more sternly at God's door than ever in closing – it's *your* wrath that has swept over me; it's *your* terrors that have destroyed me and now surround me like a flood, engulfing me; it's *you* who has taken everything away from me. This is venting at the divine at its most extreme.

Unlike every other complaint psalm, Psalm 88 does not follow the standard pattern. As already observed, there is very little being asked of God, except for in verse 2 – perhaps divine silence has put paid to such requests and all that is left to express is raw sentiment. Furthermore, there is no sense that any prayer has been heard, hence no vows that need to be repaid, nor any praise or thanksgiving that can be offered. The trust of verse 1 quickly evaporates. Instead, by the end, only divine silence and pervasive despair remain, such that 'darkness is my closest friend' (v. 18). Hopelessness appears to have the final word here, as a link is drawn, however tenuously, between God and this palpable experience of surrounding and overwhelming darkness. Nothing has changed, nothing has worked, nothing has been resolved. All the discordant notes remain.

This truly is a psalm that is unafraid to face the bare and extreme realities of life at its worst. It is surely not a psalm to be used frequently, though it has a power unlike any other to speak into those limit-experiences on the brink of existence. The speech is angry and emotive, venting and accusatory; yet crucially it maintains a conversation with God, however one-sided, even in a place of utter despair. It appears from this psalm that there is no speech that cannot be directed towards God – the message seems to be, 'Even when life hits its worst, don't stop talking to God. You can say anything, just say something.' Silence of course has its place, as we will explore shortly, when the silence of God is mirrored by our own. Yet just as we never fall completely silent, so Psalm 88 implores us to keep directing ourselves at God, even as our speech is angry, bleak and incoherent.

New Testament – John the Baptist
(Matthew 11:1–19; 14:1–12)

John the Baptist would have fitted naturally into the metaphor of the wilderness within the scheme of this book. However, we explore him here because, while John intentionally sought out the desert, he would later experience the pit, even though the latter was far from where he would have chosen to be.

In all of the gospels, John's desert ministry is the precursor to Jesus' public ministry. The prophets in the Bible were unafraid to challenge God's people, especially those in power. They insisted that God's ways were not our ways, and that God's thoughts were not our thoughts (Isaiah 55:8–9). Because of this, they often offended many. Prophets had been rare in Israel for some 400 years; however, John the Baptist swept on to the scene at the beginning of the gospels with his call to repentance. Just like Elijah before him, there is little biography or background information shared – he is suddenly there and centre stage.

A tough and eccentric character, John operated in the desert of Judea. His message to the people was clear – that this was the time for Israel's exile to finally come to an end, and that the way of the Lord was to be made clear. John was striking in both his clothing – camel's hair with a leather belt around his waist – and his diet – locusts and wild honey. However, he reserved his strongest words for Israel's leaders, the Pharisees and Sadducees. Religious observance and religious pedigree are not enough. Orthodoxy is not sufficient. To be Abraham's seed does not cover it. Without heartfelt repentance, there can be no spiritual life for you in the kingdom of the Messiah. People do not know how to handle prophets, then and now. A prophetic voice is usually an embarrassment, rarely welcomed within the walls of the establishment. As Frederick Buechner expressed it, 'There is no evidence to suggest that anyone ever asked a prophet home for supper more than once.'[4] John the Baptist played his role to perfection.

John baptised Jesus, but was arrested soon after (Matthew 4:12), having publicly rebuked Herod Antipas, ruler of Galilee, for his extra-marital affairs (Matthew 14:3–5). Herod had visited his brother in Rome and seduced his brother's wife. He had then divorced his own wife and lured his sister-in-law to leave her husband and marry him. John had paid the penalty for denouncing this behaviour – prison in the fortress of Machaerus within the burning mountains by the Dead Sea. There in the pit, he began to have questions and doubts about Jesus. John, who had devoted his whole life to preparing Israel for the coming of Jesus; who had baptised Jesus, hearing the voice from heaven affirming Jesus as God's Son and seeing the Holy Spirit descending upon him as a dove; who had pointed to Jesus and proclaimed, 'Behold! the Lamb of God who takes away the sins of the world!' – this John was now in prison, doubting and needing reassurance.

Strange as it may seem, this should be of great encouragement to us. If someone as 'strong' as John can question things, so can we. It is surely not surprising that John had his doubts in a place such as this. In the pit, our minds play tricks on us. Our thoughts can easily swirl about and quickly sink down. Doubts can grow in the toxic soil that the pit provides in abundance. Everything tends to lose shape and proportion when you are suffering for a long time in a confined space – either physically or metaphorically. No one sits in the pit and imagines that this was the way that life was meant to be. In this whirling mix, there is usually a painful sense of disappointment, not only with the circumstance but also with God.

Tom Wright observes that it was as though John had been rehearsing for a performance for years, but the star of the show had suddenly changed the script at the last moment without telling anyone.[5] John had expected Jesus to be a man of fire – an Elijah-like character who would sweep through Israel and deal with her contemporary equivalent of the prophets of Baal. No doubt John had looked forward to the day when Jesus would confront Herod, topple him from his throne and become king in his place. Alongside this, Jesus would surely get his cousin out of prison and perhaps even reward him with a place of honour. Yet Jesus appeared to be going about things in a very different way to how John had expected. Jesus did not appear to be bringing an axe to the root of trees like Herod at all. Was Jesus really the Messiah, then, or should everyone now switch tack and look elsewhere for their hope? It wasn't just that the show for which John had spent all of his life preparing was no longer going according to (his) script; more than this, it was that John no longer recognised the performance at all. In this confusion, however, John does two helpful things.

First, John shares his doubts with those around him, his disciples. Our thoughts are never more dangerous than when they swirl around endlessly in our own heads. Life takes turns that we would never have imagined and which we never would have permitted if the story had been ours to write. We try to make sense of how it ever came to this and what this tells us about God. We long to regain control of the narrative. However, without the perspective of others, we can all too easily turn in on ourselves in ways that are unhealthy. We need the perspective of others, both to encourage and to challenge, where appropriate.

Second, John takes his doubts straight to Jesus. Just as we are invited to direct everything to God in the model of the complaint psalms, so John does the same with Jesus. He cannot go to Jesus himself, so he sends word by his disciples. Jesus' answer to John makes clear that what Jesus is doing is the fulfilment of messianic passages from the Old Testament, such as Isaiah 35:5–6 and Isaiah 61:1. If the blind receive sight, the lame walk, the deaf hear and the poor have the good news preached to them, is it not clear that God's Spirit is upon Jesus, and that he is the one for whom John has been waiting?

We never find out how John responded. We don't know if this communication from Jesus was enough to lift John from his pit of despair, even as he remained physically imprisoned by Herod. If John did hold on to a narrative of his own making, he stood to sink further, for events were about to take an even darker turn. At a shady, sleazy party, Herod ended up promising what he had not intended, and John was beheaded (Matthew 14:6–12). How could things have come to this for the greatest prophet that Israel had seen before the coming of the kingdom of heaven? Or did Jesus' response reassure John that, although the story was far from what John had expected, still, in ways he couldn't comprehend, it would be greater than he could ever have imagined because it told of a 'better resurrection' (Hebrews 11:35)?

Jesus Christ – placed in the tomb

The space between is a painful time in our lives because it marks such a clear and obvious loss of control. It indicates a movement from action to passion – from where we are able to decide and do ourselves, to where other people or circumstances appear to take the initiative from us.[6] Sometimes, we experience this move from action to passion as a temporary interruption in the flow of life. As we get older, it becomes more and more integrated into the very make-up of our existence. A woman in later life in a church I know has fulfilled nearly every role going, and she is now struggling with being unable to carry on doing things. She can only imagine vocation as something involving action, not passion. It is of great consolation to us that Jesus Christ, God incarnate, knew well this move from action to passion, and that this for him was not just a temporary aberration, nor even a small detour, but a core element in the story of salvation.

The first part of Jesus' life is filled with activity. Jesus takes all sorts of initiatives – he speaks, he preaches, he heals, he travels. At the beginning of Mark's gospel especially, you are struck by the whirlwind of activity that is the arrival of Jesus upon the public scene. Following the imprisonment of John the Baptist, which appears to be a cue for Jesus' public ministry to move up a level, Jesus announces that 'the time has come' and shares good news of the kingdom being near, that all might turn and believe it. Armed with this message, he walks beside the Sea of Galilee and calls Simon and his brother Andrew to come and follow him. They go further on and he summons James, son of Zebedee, and his brother John to do the same. They head to Capernaum, where Jesus teaches in the synagogue with striking authority. Jesus exorcises an evil spirit from a man there, and news about him spreads fast. They leave the synagogue and head to the home of Simon and Andrew, where Simon's mother-in-law is in bed with a fever. Jesus helps her to her feet, the fever leaves her and she waits on them all. Then, in the evening, the ill and demon-possessed are brought to Jesus and he heals their diseases and drives out their demons.

This is merely the first day of Jesus' public ministry, as narrated by Mark! Not least in that gospel, everything moves with great pace, action and adventure. However, there comes a point in the story of Jesus where the move from action to passion begins. In the previous chapter we explored the scene of Jesus in the garden of Gethsemane, and in that drama there is a key phrase that bridges this transition. It is the phrase 'gave him over', as Jesus is betrayed by Judas, or 'given over' by him, to the chief priests as had been arranged (Mark 14:11; the word in the Greek is *paradidōmi*). After Jesus is 'handed over', he becomes the one to whom things are done. He's arrested. He's taken to the high priest. He's crowned with thorns. He's nailed to a cross. The things that he used to be able to do, he can no longer do. The agency and freedom he used to have are gone. Things are being done to him over which he has no control. This all comes to a climax in an often neglected but vital part of the gospel story in his being laid in the tomb. Things were being done to Jesus while he was alive, yet here something is done to Jesus as he is dead (Mark 15:42–47).

The burial of Jesus is a key element in the gospel story, even though Jesus was not aware of it. For Paul in 1 Corinthians 15:3–5, the burial is one of the four central, historical, physical and biblical truths of the good news. It is vital because the empty tomb is one of the main reasons we can place so much confidence in the resurrection of Jesus Christ. The disciples could not have preached about Jesus' rising from the dead if they knew that the tomb was not empty – to have done so would have been farcical. Moreover, the knowledge that the tomb was empty relies itself on the prior knowledge of where Jesus' body was laid in the first place. The gospels make clear that Jesus' body was taken by Joseph of Arimathea, who was a member of the Jewish

Sanhedrin (Mark 15:43; Matthew 27:57; Luke 23:50–56) and who buried Jesus in a tomb that he owned. This is reported in very early sources and is described by John A.T. Robinson as 'one of the earliest and best-attested facts about Jesus'.[7] Yet, in all that takes place here, Jesus is passive in the extreme.

The wonder of the working of God is that Jesus doesn't only fulfil his vocation in his action but also in his passion. Jesus is faithful to the Father and available as a vessel to be used by him not merely in all he does, but in all that is done to him as well. Even in death, God's purposes prevail through Jesus. Stunningly, Romans 8:32 uses the same word in the Greek to describe God's action in salvation as Mark does for Judas – *paradidōmi*, 'gave him over' – 'He who did not with-hold his own Son, but gave him up for all of us, will he not with him also give us everything else?' (NRSV). For surely *this* is the power of God – that he can work *all* things together for good, both our action *and* our passion; both the things that we do *and* the things that are done to us. Because of this, even our loss of control in the space between becomes holy ground on which God can work, since 'we know that in all things God works for the good of those who love him, who have been called according to his purpose' (Romans 8:28).

Sacred time – Holy Saturday

Holy Saturday is the space between the horror of Good Friday and the glory of Easter Sunday. It's the day that is often confused – it isn't Easter Saturday – or, worse still, forgotten. As A.J. Swoboda notes:

> Christians defend certain days of the Holy Weekend. For instance, we'll defend the idea that on Friday Jesus actually dies on a cross to save the world from its sin. Then we'll turn around and defend Easter Sunday as the day that Jesus actually rose from the grave… But nobody defends Saturday. Nobody writes apologetics defending the belief that Jesus actually lay dead for one long, endless day two thousand years ago.[8]

Churches often mark Maundy Thursday, Good Friday and Easter Sunday, but in this most momentous of weekends, Holy Saturday will rarely be mentioned. This is a great loss because it is the day that is truer to our everyday reality of life than any other. It perfectly embodies liminal space, caught between the sorrow of Good Friday and the celebration of Easter Sunday. Christians are sometimes spoken of as 'Easter people'. For sure, that is the hope to which we are headed. Yet, for now, on this side of eternity, we are far more 'Holy Saturday people'. This isn't as catchy, yet it holds the tension and awkwardness that we often feel in our lives of faith between great despair and overwhelming hope.

On Holy Saturday we experience the silence and the stillness of this 'time out of time' as earth awaits the resurrection. It all seems so bleak. We pinch ourselves to check whether yesterday really did happen. There are no sacraments, there is no light and no warmth, and we can do nothing. It is as though life itself were suspended. This is a unique aspect of Christianity. 'Only Christianity insists that a legitimate stage of holiness is hopelessness.'[9] Saturday was the day of the Jewish sabbath. Jesus had completed his work (John 19:30) and, like his Father, was now resting. The Jewish sabbath was a day full of hope and longing for the future: a day to look forward with anticipation to the time when God does indeed make all things new. As one person has put it, 'Even resurrection pauses for sabbath rest.'[10]

So what, if anything, do Christians think was going on during Holy Saturday? This is the day when God alone acts – powerfully, redemptively – behind the scenes. The Apostle's Creed says that Jesus descended into hell, and therefore many theologians argue that Holy Saturday was the day when Jesus, as the righteous one, broke open the power of hell. For others, it wasn't so much hell but Hades, the place of the dead, that Jesus went to. In accordance with Acts 2:31, 1 Peter 3:18–19 suggests that Jesus 'was put to death in the body but made alive in the Spirit. After being made alive, he went and made proclamation to the imprisoned spirits.' These references and others (Matthew 12:40; 27:51–52; 1 Peter 4:6; Ephesians 4:9; Revelation 20:14) provide the origins for the church's idea of the 'harrowing of hell', more common in the Eastern Orthodox Church, in which Jesus is 'striding victoriously into hell and reaching out in love even to the dead and the damned'.[11] Its continuing importance is to tell us that there is no place in which God is not present.

There is a powerful principle at work here, which runs through the entire theme of the space between, and which can be found throughout the scriptures: the revelation of the hiddenness of the kingdom of God. The kingdom of God is in our midst, yet it is also likened to a mustard seed, which is too small to notice. One day it may grow into a huge tree, yet for now it is out of sight. The kingdom is found in Lazarus begging at the rich man's gate, in the child at the margins while the adults are talking, in the slave who is washing your feet – though few have eyes to see. And so, even in the silence, there is still hope. Epiphanius, Bishop of Cyprus (AD403), put it this way in an ancient homily: 'Something strange is happening – there is a great silence on earth today, a great silence and stillness. The whole earth keeps silence because the King is asleep.'

Sacred practice – silence

In the pit, prayer is bleak, as in Psalm 88, and it can quickly fall silent. Words fail us. We may have tried to think and to rationalise ourselves out of the situation, but here we are, sunk down in darkness. Perhaps our prayers came with words in better times, though what words can be articulated now? Where feelings before may have been raw, now they can just feel numb. God is on mute. We fall silent too. All too often, we can use words to express (false) certainty. However, the surprising truth is that our wordless prayers may be some of the most profound ones that we will ever pray. Tom Wright goes so far as to say, 'At the very moment when we are struggling to pray, and have no idea even what to pray for, just at that point the Spirit is most obviously at work'.[12] Romans 8:26–27 offers a powerful and profound encouragement for those who have come to the end of human language in their praying:

In the same way, the Spirit helps us in our weakness. We do not know what we ought to pray for, but the Spirit himself intercedes for us through wordless groans. And he who searches our hearts knows the mind of the Spirit, because the Spirit intercedes for God's people in accordance with the will of God.

The previous verses have recognised a world in deep pain, groaning for the coming of a new creation. The church is not apart from this pain but shares in it, caught in the eschatological space between: we possess the first fruits of the Spirit and yet are stuck in our present mortal existence. The Spirit calls out of us a groaning that cannot be put into words. Wright goes on to: 'This is prayer beyond prayer, diving down into the cold, dark depths beyond human sight or knowing' – yet not beyond the God whom Wright in his translation calls 'the Searcher of Hearts'. God understands what the Spirit is saying, even if we do not. God hears and answers the very prayers that we might be in danger of dismissing as lacking substance – those painful groanings, the tossings and turnings of an unquiet spirit. For in the pit, this may be all that we can offer to God. The good news is that it is all that is needed. Amid the disquiet, there is a paradoxical invitation to come to a place where we can obey the instruction of Psalm 46:10 – 'Be still, and know that I am God.' Apophatic prayer, or the practice of silent prayer, can help us to do this.

We are all accustomed to cataphatic theology – whether we're familiar with the term or not. This is any positive affirmation of who and what God is. We describe God as our 'rock' and our 'saviour', or say that 'God is love', and in doing so we are using cataphatic, or positive, terms. Apophatic theology[13] is sometimes called negative theology, though this resonance doesn't do it justice. It's the idea that we reach a certain point in our knowledge of God where we need to step into paradox – the acceptance that it is only through *not* knowing that God can fill us with a deeper knowledge of who he is. This doesn't negate the scriptural affirmations that we know and love, but it does bring an acknowledgement that even our understanding of these comes from preconceived ideas, beliefs and biases, of which we may not be aware. Instead, there is a recognition that:

'My thoughts are not your thoughts, neither are your ways my ways,' declares the Lord. 'As the heavens are higher than the earth, so are my ways higher than your ways and my thoughts than your thoughts.'

ISAIAH 55:8–9

In intentionally practising silence, it is important to find a place of stillness in which to sit. Choosing a designated part of the house to keep coming back to and cultivating this space can be helpful. This becomes our 'cell' – in the monastic rather than imprisoned sense of the word. In this place, it's good to sit comfortably in a way that enables us to relax – posture is important. Some find it helpful to have an 'anchor word' to come back to – 'God', 'Jesus', 'Spirit', 'love' or 'joy' – as a way of staying focused; or a prayer, such as, 'Here I am, Lord. I long to meet with you' or the 'Jesus Prayer', to keep repeating. We can be conscious of our breathing, in and out – slowing it down and letting this become an expression of our prayer. In the same way that no one goes 'from couch to 5K' in one session, we should start small, setting a timer for just a few minutes, and building up gradually from there. We don't need to 'achieve' anything in the time – it is simply an offering to God. Sometimes it can be easier to share silence with others – this may not seem to make sense, yet the experience is very powerful. Interestingly, during the Covid-19 lockdowns, I've read of people from all walks of life connecting with one another on Zoom simply to share silence and community together as they work.

In the monastic tradition, 'cell' is the foundational space that flows out to all the other sacred spaces in our lives.[14] This is because cell is unavoidably the place where we are confronted with ourselves – again, 'Go, sit in your cell, and your cell will teach you everything.' However, cell, with its practice of stillness, is the place of transformation precisely because it is where we stop trying to control the world with our words, thoughts and ideas, and can finally be still and know God.

The Christian practice of the night-time vigil, especially on Christmas Eve or Easter Eve, is another powerful expression of silence. Prayer vigils in the night are an early Christian practice which have been sustained through the ages. The power of sitting in the silence of the night, with a candle lit, waiting for the dawn, is an unimaginably poignant expression of hope. Culturally, we see it demonstrated whenever tragedy strikes and people instinctively light a candle and wait in the darkness, often with others and usually in silence. Intuitively, as Psalm 139:7–12 expresses, there is a knowledge that, even in the darkness, we cannot escape God's presence:

Where can I go from your Spirit?
  Where can I flee from your presence?
If I go up to the heavens, you are there;
  if I make my bed in the depths, you are there.
If I rise on the wings of the dawn,
  if I settle on the far side of the sea,
even there your hand will guide me,
  your right hand will hold me fast.
If I say, 'Surely the darkness will hide me
  and the light become night around me,'
even the darkness will not be dark to you;
  the night will shine like the day,
  for darkness is as light to you.

Sacred stories

Historical saints – Terry Waite and John of the Cross

Terry Waite

One of my strongest memories of watching the news growing up was the capture of Terry Waite. In the 1980s, Waite was the assistant for Anglican Communion affairs for the Archbishop of Canterbury Robert Runcie. As an envoy for the Church of England, he successfully negotiated the release of several hostages in Iran, Libya and Lebanon.

In 1987, he travelled again to Lebanon to try to secure the freedom of four hostages, including the journalist John McCarthy, but was himself kidnapped and taken captive. As part of this, he was interrogated, tortured and subjected to a mock execution. His captivity lasted 1,763 days, the first four years of which were spent in solitary confinement. He was finally released on 18 November 1991. Miraculously, Waite was able to resist bitterness, observing, much like Mandela, 'If you are bitter, it will eat you up and do you much more damage than the people who have hurt you.'[15]

Waite says that his Anglican faith remained intact while in captivity, although he didn't find it to be a 'profound spiritual experience', nor claim to 'feel the close presence of God' in that time. 'Feelings can be distorted in all sorts of ways – illness can distort feeling, situations and so on. If you make faith dependent on feeling you can so easily be led astray.' Part of the gift of the space between, if it can be seen in this way, is to break our common tendency to over-connect our feelings about God with the apparent strength, or weakness, of our faith. Faith goes far deeper than our feelings.

It's fascinating to reflect on what sustained Waite during his time in captivity. He says that he had no conscious memory whatsoever of the many sermons he had sat through – a great encouragement to all of us who preach! – but that, instead, it was the language of the Psalms and the Book of Common Prayer that became a well for him to draw from. The power of scripture, good liturgy and good music cannot be overstated. The internet offers us access to more information than we can possibly comprehend, yet this can never replace the importance of committing scripture especially to memory. This reminds me of the importance of both formality and informality in our devotions, of both set prayer and extempore prayer. The freedom of the latter is a wonderful gift that I have always appreciated. Yet I notice that in the toughest of times in my life, when my own words run out, I need to draw from the deposit of set words that have been honed and crafted through the ages, as well as to embrace the gift of silence.

In 2008, Waite became a member of the Society of Friends, or the Quakers. He jokes about calling himself a 'Quanglican'. Waite had always been impressed by the ethical position the Quakers upheld, including their championing of just business practices. However, it was only when he experienced almost five years of solitary confinement as a hostage that he 'caught a glimmer of the spiritual heart of the movement'.[16] Waite has subsequently come to experience the beauty and spiritual depth of a Quaker meeting where corporate silence is held together. He reminds us of the importance of space for silent reflection and contemplation in our own gatherings, whatever tradition we may be from.

In spite of a lack of 'feeling' or 'experience' in captivity, Waite demonstrates the potential of the space between to shape us: 'Ultimately, suffering – in the majority of cases – needn't destroy. Something creative can emerge from it.'

John of the Cross

The cause of Terry Waite's experience of the pit was obvious. However, with St John of the Cross, things can be far more enigmatic during a 'dark night of the soul'.

John was born in Castile, Spain, and became a Carmelite monk in 1564. In 1567, he met with Teresa of Ávila and she put him in charge of the order, admiring his skills of leadership and his rigorous lifestyle. It was during this time that he was named 'John of the Cross' as a result of his suffering and commitment. He continued to harness his gifts for the benefit of the Catholic Reformation, both in terms of his leadership and his many writings. He was eventually arrested and put in confinement by those who opposed the reform. It was here that he wrote his most famous work, 'The Dark Night of the Soul'. This concept of a 'dark night' has become an integral part of understanding the spiritual journey for many and continues to exercise great influence today.

John's revelation was that, at a certain point in their spiritual journey, God will draw a person from a stage of beginning to a more advanced stage. This is like the move from milk to solids in a baby. To stay on milk would be a strange sign of failing to grow up. Richard Foster writes that 'to desire spiritual maturity without the dark night is like an athlete hoping to become a champion without training or an author expecting to produce a book without thinking'.[17] As God leads a person to go deeper in their spiritual life, they will likely experience this 'dark night of the soul', in which they lose all the pleasure they had once experienced in their life in God. God will feel distant, but for no discernible reason. However, the results of this work are profound. The dark night helps us to be free from the seven capital sins – pride, wrath, greed, lust, gluttony, envy and sloth – and develops in us seven contrasting great virtues – humility, patience, generosity, chastity, peace, kindness and diligence. The dark night is one of the key means that God uses for our transformation.

The revelation of the dark night of the soul is profound, yet it can be misread and misunderstood. It is not just that bad things might happen to us or that we might feel down – though the phrase has understandably been taken to refer to such trials. Rather, it refers to the person who is earnestly seeking God, who has known the joy of their salvation, but who now, for no reason they can see, finds no sustenance in their devotional walk. It takes seriously the challenge of a dedicated and disciplined spiritual life, that even this can be a source of idolatry. It is a powerful corrective to our modern spiritual tendencies. We may recognise the dangers of a 'health and wealth' gospel, yet most of us can fall into an implicit assumption that if God feels distant then something must be wrong. It challenges our modern consumerist spiritualities that are all about our being fed. The trouble is, feasting when you're not hungry can sometimes be unhealthy. Here, it is as though God starves us for a time to make us hunger for him again.

Contemporary saint

This is the story, in their own words, of a friend who has journeyed, or is still journeying, through the space between.

Pits are lonely places. Inviting light into that darkness is terrifying. Honest evaluation is hard work.

It seemed impossible to be free of the reality I was living – like a prison where the key had been thrown away. I believed I had exhausted all efforts for change, but change never came; and the toxicity of my environment remained the same. I felt as if I couldn't breathe. God was very much a part of my life; however, my relationship with him and the church was very much lived in the third person. I was outside looking in – reading and believing God's word, but believing it was true for everyone else. 'Jesus has come to give abundant life' and 'Nothing can separate you from God's love' were words I often heard, but I did not believe them to be true for me. I spent a long time attempting to figure out why my circumstances remained. I spent a long time fighting to change them, but years of unanswered prayers and fruitless fighting produced a heavy weariness. I knew the words to say and the way to act to appear happy and whole, but my internal emptiness betrayed my outward act, and I grew numb. I felt nothing. That numbness scared me. Growing apathetic to life was the antithesis of the love upon which the foundation of my faith was supposed to be built, and this realisation was the catalyst that moved me to seek help beyond myself.

The climb out of the pit would have been impossible without help. Hard questions were asked; deep insight was provided. Trusted friends gathered to support me when I couldn't stand on my own. So much I believed about life changed. Unhealthy understandings of God and faith crumbled and were rebuilt upon first-person realities. I was no longer on the outside looking in. I was experiencing God myself, beginning to truly understand that I was not outside the boundaries of his love. He was no longer an impersonal God working all things for good for others; he was living and active in my life.

The journey out has been difficult. Many times I felt I would be crushed under the weight of the burden, but each step forward produced a new strength. The letting-go and crumbling of old ideas, unhealthy thoughts and life circumstances produced a chaotic ruin, but old things must be torn down to make room for the new. In Christ, death brings life. I'm still in the midst of my climb. Some days are harder than others. Pits leave lasting impressions on our souls – like scars. They will heal, but a reminder will always remain. I'm so thankful for that scar. It reminds me that I've walked through that notorious valley of the shadow of death, and he was with me. He is with me. I am no longer numb. The journey out is difficult, but it is worth each step. True and abundant life is on the other side.

'Lament Psalm One' by Ann Weems

O God, have you forgotten my name?
How long will you leave me
In this pit?
I sang hosannas
All the days of my life
And waved palm branches
Greened in the new spring world.
Rich only in promises
From you,
I followed
Believing,
And then they killed him
Whom I loved
More than my own life
(even that you taught me).
They killed him
Whom you gave to me.
They killed him
Without a thought
For justice or mercy,

And I sit now in darkness
Hosannas stuck in my throat…

Why should I wave palm branches
Or look for Easter mornings?
O God, why did you name me Rachel?
A cry goes up out of Ramah,
And it is my cry!
Rachel will not be comforted!
Don't you hear me,
You whose name is Emmanuel?
Won't you come to me? How long must I wait
On this bed of pain
Without a candle
To ward off the night?
Come, Holy One,
Feed to me a taste of your shalom.
Come, lift to my lips
A cup of cold water
That I might find my voice
To praise you
Here in the pit.
Pull forth the hosannas
From my parched lips,
And I will sing to all
Of your everlasting goodness,
For then the world will know that My God is a God of promise
Who comes to me
In my darkness.
Ann Weems[18]

Questions for reflection

1 What would you say has been the darkest moment of your life so far? Are you able to express anything of this in word or image?
2 How do you react to the bleakness of Psalm 88? Does it depress you or console you? What else in the chapter might offer chinks of light for times of darkness?
3 What is the place of silence and the 'apophatic' for you at present? Can you make more room for this?

8

Conclusion

He will wipe every tear from their eyes. There will be no more death or mourning or crying or pain, for the old order of things has passed away.
REVELATION 21:4

The good news comes knocking on doors that we didn't even know we had; it flings open the curtains on windows we didn't know existed to reveal the rising sun flooding the room with glory when we had imagined that all light came from candles; it woos our cold hearts and awakens them, like someone falling in love for the first time, to a joy and fulfillment never before imagined.[1]

Psalms 42 and 43

Psalms 42 and 43 bring together our five different perspectives on the space between in a powerful way. They embrace a waiting for God (42:2), an experience of exile (42:6), the dryness of the desert (42:1–2), the force of the storm (42:7) and the darkness of the pit (43:3). It is likely that Psalms 42 and 43 once belonged together. This is evident from the refrain that reoccurs in 42:5, 11 and 43:5. Perhaps the reason for the separation at one stage in time was the slightly different focuses of the two psalms.

Psalm 42 is like a journal entry in which the psalmist speaks to themself, recording the narrative of their soul's journey. The practice of journalling is highly recommended in the space between. It is important to try to give voice to our experiences, even as they lack coherence and cannot be put into what might feel like meaningful language. Yet they do need to come out to avoid swirling around our minds, completely unprocessed. Psalm 42 is the psalmist seeking to give voice to the swathe of contradictions that their life has become. Psalm 43 picks up from Psalm 42 and pursues the story more directly with God before concluding with the same refrain.

In the refrain, the psalmist speaks to their soul, longing to move beyond their present situation of feeling downcast and disturbed. The psalmist wills their soul to embrace a future that will surely come, it seems, by putting their hope in God. Though mired in despair at present, there is the belief that praise will yet arise. As with Jacob at Bethel, there is a personal claiming of God as *my* Saviour and *my* God. How paradoxically intimate the space between can be for this most vital of all our relationships.

The first stanza of Psalm 42 comes in verses 1–4. The psalmist is dried up, panting for an encounter with God that will water their present barrenness. The promise of Isaiah 55 is that anyone in such a place need only come to the waters and drink, yet here the psalmist's bitter tears flow to provide their only source of nourishment. The psalmist's own longing to meet with God and their questioning of when they can do this again are exacerbated by the taunts of others as to where God might be in the midst of their suffering. As with Hannah (1 Samuel 1:15), however, these taunts lead the psalmist to pour out their soul. Past encounters are remembered, which must rub salt into the wound; yet at the same time these provide the hope of fresh encounter, as we saw in Psalm 63. Now God is absent, but then the psalmist knew his protection; now there are tears and lament, but then there were shouts of joy and praise; now the psalmist is alone, but then they were among the festive throng.

In the second stanza (vv. 6–10), the experience of feeling downcast triggers a further bout of remembrance. Jerusalem and the temple were the centre of worship for Israel, yet the foothills of Mount Hermon are as far away from Jerusalem as you can be in Israel (this is the region known as Caesarea Philippi in the gospels). The psalmist is cut off, or exiled, from the place where they long to dwell. These foothills of Mount Hermon are where the waters of the Jordan burst from the mountain, and this provides an image for the way things can overwhelm us – they are like a storm, like huge waves that crash over us. The poet who desperately sought water at the beginning of the psalm now finds it in abundance, yet in a destructive, rather than life-giving, form. The waters are interpreted as God's waves, which may be problematic, though might be a source of hope in that, since they are God's waves, they are under his control. As the stanza goes on, there is a real conflict of emotions – both an intimate sense of the presence of God (v. 8) yet also a keen sense of his absence (vv. 9–10).

All of this comes to a head in Psalm 43. In 42:9, we had a report of speech *to* God; here we have the live event. The *internal* monologue of lament is turned into *external* speech to God – the inward reflection and dwelling on memory at last becomes an outward plea as the psalmist finds their voice. It is this change that seems to be the beginning of progress for the psalmist. There is a new-found confidence in verses 1–2 for God to deliver and to defend. Out of this there is fresh hope for a leading out of darkness and a journey to Jerusalem for fresh encounter with God. Whereas in Psalm 42 the praise of God was only a distant memory, now in Psalm 43:4 it is a future vow – it can be imagined again. When the refrain returns at the end, it is the hope and vow that now feel more dominant than the feelings of being downcast and disturbed.

There is a beautiful portrayal in these psalms of the aching pain of the struggle in the psalmist's soul. Their longing for God acts as a power that sustains them through fear and torment, doubt and temptation, until those forces are overcome by faith and waiting for God.

Our liminal existence – time, space and matter

The more I reflect on the disruptive and liminal moments in our lives, the more I see just how important they are. This is surely because, when we break it down theologically, all of our existence of *time*, *space* and *matter* is presently one of liminality and of being 'caught between'.

In relation to *time*, we are 'caught between the ages'. The Jewish expectation of a messianic 'age to come', to bring to an end 'this present age', has been fulfilled in Jesus Christ. His kingdom has broken into this world, such that on the cross, he conquered sin and death and all the powers of this world. And yet, we find that so much of the pain, hurt and suffering of our world is still in operation. In Christ, the 'age to come' has begun; at the same time, we continue to live within 'this present age'. Our current existence, therefore, takes place in the overlap of the ages: living in the present, but longing for a future that is coming.

We find also that the *space* in which we live is caught itself in a liminal place. Paul writes that even creation is in a state of travail, groaning as in the pains of childbirth for what it longs to become (Romans 8:22–25). Such travail will only be released when Christ appears again, when judgement comes, and when all of creation can be put to rights. Such a day is wonderfully imagined by John the Seer at the close of the book of Revelation:

> Then I saw 'a new heaven and a new earth,' for the first heaven and the first earth had passed away, and there was no longer any sea. I saw the Holy City, the new Jerusalem, coming down out of heaven from God, prepared as a bride beautifully dressed for her husband. And I heard a loud voice from the throne saying, 'Look! God's dwelling-place is now among the people, and he will dwell with them. They will be his people, and God himself will be with them and be their God. "He will wipe every tear from their eyes.

There will be no more death" or mourning or crying or pain, for the old order of things has passed away.' He who was seated on the throne said, 'I am making everything new!'
REVELATION 21:1–5

Within this context of time and space, even the *matter* of our own existence is in a liminal state. Our bodies are subject to decay, corruption and failure; yet, at the same time, God has set eternity in our hearts (Ecclesiastes 3:11). More than this, he has raised Christ, as the prototype of all that we are to become. If Christ has been raised from the dead, then all who are in Christ will on the last day be raised as well – not to some purely spiritual bliss, but to a fully embodied life within the renewed creation that God will bring to reality. Quite what all this will look like, we can only imagine. For example, the risen Christ was clearly embodied: walking, talking, eating and drinking with the disciples, and yet he was able to come and go at will, passing through even locked doors! Surely, the best any of us can do is to agree with the words of the apostle John when he says, 'Dear friends, now we are children of God, and what we will be has not yet been made known. But we know that when Christ appears, we shall be like him, for we shall see him as he is' (1 John 3:2).

In the light of the liminality of our current existence, in terms of time, space and matter, it is no surprise that the disruptive moments of our lives have such an important role to play.

Disruption, reimagination, transformation

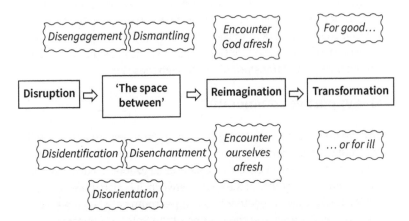

We have explored how seasons of disruption lead us into the liminality of the space between. In these times, we are forced to leave behind the old, though are not yet able to lay hold of the new. We find ourselves caught 'betwixt and between', feeling as though we are neither in one place nor another. This loss of the known world is a deeply painful thing: we feel a separation from what has gone before (disengagement); the structures that used to hold life together are coming apart (dismantling); our sense of ourselves and who we are is in flux (disidentification); we may feel let down and disillusioned with the world, others, ourselves and even God (disenchantment); and in all of this we can feel bewildered and lost (disorientation).

As painful as this may seem, however, the space between is a profound opportunity for transformation. In the words of Richard Rohr, quoted in the introduction:

> Nothing good or creative emerges from business as usual. This is why much of the work of God is to get people into liminal space, and to keep them there long enough so they can learn something essential. It is the ultimate teachable space… maybe the only one.[2]

We can be sure that the space between will be transformative and that, most likely, it will leave its mark on us forever. However, whether this is for good or for ill can depend on how we partner with the grace of God that is at work in these seasons. The following postures, or practices, offer good soil for God to plant seeds in us that can bring about a harvest of transformation through these times.[3]

1 Supportive community

We are never fully in control of this, yet as far as we are able we will need to seek out, and be open to, supportive community around us. The model is there in Luke 1 as Zechariah, Elizabeth, Mary, Simeon and Anna wait together in the space between. It is also there in Acts 1 as the disciples wait together in the upper room between the ascension of Jesus Christ and the coming of the Spirit at Pentecost. We long for these models of community in our lives and not those of Job, who was poorly served by the friends around him. We will need to exercise grace with those around us. They cannot know what we are feeling, even as we are not sure ourselves some of the time. Those in our circles who have been through seasons of intense disruption, liminality and loss will know something of what is needed at times like this, while others may offer their best yet sometimes miss the mark.

However, even if such people cannot be found, we are never alone. God promises to be with us always (Matthew 28:20), never to leave us nor forsake us (Hebrews 13:5), and assures us that we can never be separated from his love (Romans 8:38–39). We are also being cheered on by a 'great cloud of witnesses' (Hebrews 12:1) – that communion of saints who have gone before us and are now rooting for us. We only need the eyes of faith to see that there are more championing our cause than we could ever have imagined (2 Kings 6:16).

2 Intentional solitude

There is a paradox here in that, while we do need the support of others around us, by itself this will not be enough to lead us through these times. There is inner work that we alone can do and which we ourselves must take responsibility for. Time and space alone allows us to deal with what's inside of us, rather than seeking to numb it or avoid it. Different people will process this in different ways – for example, regular times of quiet, physical exercise, long walks and retreat space are all possibilities. As with the community we seek to put around us, the intentionality of our solitude can be important.

3 Painful honesty

In our experience of loss, we can be left in a nothingness when there are few answers and many questions. Caught up in the pain of 'dying', it can feel as though there is precious little hope for living. Honesty in three ways will be important.

First, *honesty with ourselves*. The space between is always a bewildering time, so attempting to process it by journalling can be helpful. This is about slowing down and forcing ourselves to put things into words or pictures, however inadequate these may seem. It involves considering what is really going on, how we are feeling and why this might be so, and where we discern God to be in the midst of everything. This isn't a looking for 'the answer' – it's much deeper than that.

Second, and most importantly, *honesty with God*. The biblical reality is that we are invited to bring ourselves, exactly as we are, before God in prayer and relationship. God longs that we share the brutal facts with him – the unfiltered truth – rather than a carefully processed and edited version of this. The psalms of lament, or complaint, offer us the perfect model for doing this.

Third, *honesty with others*. We do well to share life with people who seek to listen to us, and who will support us and encourage us along the way. Equally, there can be the challenge here of letting our walls down and allowing others in, given the ache of what we feel.

No one can practise this threefold painful honesty 24/7, however – it would be too exhausting. It is important to acknowledge that as well and to allow ourselves space to recover when we do face up to reality.

4 Disciplined patience

Things do not tend to move quickly in the space between. The resolutions that we long for can be painfully slow to appear. All of the easy answers have vanished, and we are left with a new level of intensity, unlike anything we may have experienced before. We will need patience in this season to avoid slipping into despair.

We need to come to terms with our need for this time. This involves having an understanding of exactly what it is that has brought us to this place. It may be helpful to lay out the specifics of why it is that life seems to have stalled. Bridges argues that this will help with the two temptations of the space between – fast forward and reverse. Trying to speed things up is tempting but unrealistic, and we are rarely as in control of circumstances as we would wish. Equally, we do need to keep moving somehow. We cannot go back to the way things were, as this unsettling experience is new and can only lead us to a new place, even if that is unknown at this time.

Sometimes, this phase can feel like a sinking, and the failure to find specific answers proves hopeless and impossible to live with. Expectations haven't been delivered on, and we want out. This is the point at which bitterness can set in. However, for others, the desperation can lead to a new depth and comfort in God. Answers aren't the issue anymore – what becomes important is knowing, in a new way, and apart from feelings, that above all else God is with us.

Perseverance is essential in carrying us through, as we hold fast to the grace of God. Worshipping God as a choice of our will can be vital.

Our heads may be unable to make sense of life and our hearts may not be feeling anything, yet we can still choose to turn up before God as an act of the will. This should not be misunderstood as religious or empty; rather, it is a sacrificial offering of choosing to remain in prayer in spite of the cost.

5 Reflective remembrance

The 'doorway effect' – that temporary forgetfulness as we move from room-to-room – is a well-known phenomenon. The mind empties a little as it comes to a threshold, so as to create new space for information. In the space between, this enables us to step into a deeper knowing. However, in transitional times there are some things that we must not forget, and we take confidence from the power of memory and remembrance. We may not feel God powerfully in the present, yet it can be helpful to hold on to moments of encounter with God in the past, as well as knowledge of his faithful provision in times gone by. This is an important task in helping to frame a perspective on the whole of our lives, lest the current season seeps through our imaginations to colour all that has gone before in ways that do not do it justice. Surely, this is the reason that the sons of Korah speak in Psalm 42 of remembering 'how I used to go to the house of God under the protection of the Mighty One with shouts of joy and praise among the festive throng' (v. 4) and why David in Psalm 63 calls to mind having seen God in the sanctuary and having beheld his power and his glory (v. 2). In the valley, it is vital to recall the mountaintop experiences.

It can be helpful to take this pause in the action of our lives to write something of an autobiography. Linked with the journalling, this is a slowing down to consider where life has come from and to where it might be heading. Trying to make sense of the past will help in explorations of the present, and inevitably the future as well. All of my times in the space between have triggered an almost inevitable re-evaluation of my life so far and the story that it tells.

6 Present perspective

We should also take the opportunity that the space between affords us to discover what it is that we really want in life. Life is 'vapour', as the writer of Ecclesiastes tells us – what is it that we are living for? In the usual sleepwalk of life, we can simply be getting by without ever being in touch with our deepest longings. How are we living in the deepest parts of ourselves, and is this truly the way that we seek to be? Are we doing what we believe God has set us upon this earth to do?

As strange as it might seem, it can be helpful to consider what might be 'unlived' in us were our lives to end today. One reflective exercise to this end is to imagine how our obituary might read if it were to be written at this time. What might appear to be a morbid practice can paradoxically be a transformational one for living life in more of its fullness. Famously, for Alfred Nobel it was something that changed his perspective entirely – albeit unintentionally. Alfred's brother, Ludvig, died in 1888 from a heart attack, but it was Alfred's obituary that was printed in a newspaper by mistake. It described him as the man who, through the invention of dynamite, had made it possible to kill more people more quickly than anyone who had ever lived. Shortly after this, Alfred established the Nobel Prizes for literature, peace, economics, medicine and the sciences, and this is what people know him for today.

7 Defiant hope

Most psychologists agree on the central importance of hope in life. Barbara Fredrickson puts it like this: 'Deep within the core of hope is the belief that things can change. No matter how awful or uncertain they are at the moment, things can turn out better. Possibilities exist. Hope sustains you. It keeps you from collapsing into despair.'[4]

By definition, followers of Jesus Christ are people of defiant and inescapable hope. This flows from the centrality of the resurrection of Jesus Christ to the Christian story. We have charted some of the liminal moments of the church year, beginning with the season of

Advent, and then exploring Epiphany, Lent, Good Friday and Holy Saturday. The climax of this journey is the celebration of Easter. The apostle Paul was well aware that, without the message of Easter, there could be no Christianity (1 Corinthians 15:14). However, because of its surety, the world is changed forever, and suffering and heartache can never have the final word. In Jesus Christ, the cross, which had only ever spoken of suffering and shame, came to tell instead of grace and forgiveness. In the same way, our encounters with the risen Christ, even in the space between, are able to transform sadness into hope, fear into confidence, doubt into confirmation, shattered dreams into new beginnings and failure into restoration.[5]

This book has invited us to explore five biblical metaphors of the space between as a way of framing our own experiences of disruption and liminality: the time of waiting, the place of exile, the wilderness, the storm and the pit. The reason for this is that each of these metaphors, while capturing the pain of the space between, also carries the hope of resurrection as part of the bigger story of salvation told within scripture.

Milton Friedman is surely right in saying that 'when that crisis occurs, the actions that are taken depend on the ideas that are lying around'. As followers of Jesus Christ, we have the most extraordinary ideas lying around us. We have stories in both the Old Testament and the New of those who have lived through liminal seasons of life. We have the Psalms, which provide a language of connection with God through every emotion of life. We have the seasons of the church year, which centre us on Jesus Christ and invite us to live well in disruption and liminality. We have the practices of the church, which have sustained Christians through the ages in times such as this. We have the stories of the saints – ancient and modern, and those in our own circles of family and friendship – who have wisdom to share from their own journeys. Ultimately, we have the life, death and resurrection of Jesus Christ – to which all else points – as our ultimate source of hope and life. As I shared at the beginning, my prayer with this book is that strength may be found for those times in life when it so often fails, and that hope might be glimpsed that God is strangely at work, even when he can seem to be so very far away.

8 Broken surrender

In a place beyond clear answers, rosy feelings and a keen sense of control, we come to the end of ourselves. This is a scary place, and it is no surprise that we feel as though we want to hide from it. However, here we reach the true goal of God's work in the space between. When our hands are held up in surrender, or we fall to our knees in submission, we are finally in the place where the power of God can be made known in our weakness (2 Corinthians 12:9). Such surrender is not a one-off moment, but a decision to which we keep returning. We are called to continually live in this place, and to constantly realign ourselves with God and his purposes. We come to realise, again and again, that God himself is the prize, rather than it being the answer or outcome that we have been seeking. With this, a quiet peace can descend as we look to the future with hope, even as answers remain off in the distance. Oswald Chambers famously said: 'Complete weakness and dependence will always be the occasion for the Spirit of God to manifest his power.' This is the place to which the space between can bring us – a place of weakness, dependence, surrender and submission.

9 Dependent trust

Broken surrender brings with it the fruit of a greater trust in God – in his love and faithfulness, his power and provision. This is a faith that enables us to place the full weight of our lives upon God, and which banishes fear because control has been given over to one who is greater. Our heads are lifted and our feet firmly grounded. This brings release as we hit new depths of confidence in God and learn that he is all-sufficient for our need: 'The Lord is my shepherd, I lack nothing' (Psalm 23:1). This is the 'true knowing' that covers all the 'not knowing' with which we wrestle in the space between. We can trust God for many things, but here, in closing, are three specifics.

First, we can trust that God is at work, even where we cannot see him. Mark Sayers describes the amazing response in the jungle to the felling of a tree, based on a nature documentary he watched that used time-lapse photography.[6] Specifically, he observes the space that the felling created and how this space was filled – seeing the whole thing as a parable of growth and maturity.

First, the space is quickly filled by broad-leafed plants, whose large leaves are able to capture great amounts of sunlight, which allows for rapid and spectacular growth. Then thin trees begin to break through the broad-leafed plants, but their position is precarious as threadlike vines begin to lap at the bottom of their thin and vulnerable trunks and to quickly suffocate and overwhelm them. For a time, this is all there is in the scene. Finally, a lone trunk seems to appear from nowhere and breaks through the blanket of vines. It is strong, solid and rises to the height of all the surrounding trees. It will last for centuries.

The meaning of the parable is profound. The spectacular, visible, early results of the broad-leafed plants come at the cost of leaves, roots and structure that are fragile. The trees that come through next have some success but they lack resilience. The vines are merely parasitic on the hard work of what is around them. Sayers notes how the tree that wins the race does something counter-intuitive:

> While the others fight for space, air, and light, it goes under-ground. While the others head upwards pushing through the surface, it goes deep. While the others pursue visibility at the expense of stability, the tree remains underground, hidden, building powerful roots. The deep underground foundations grown by the tree ensure that it is connected to deep and unseen sources of water, nutrients, and life. Once these are secured, growth can then happen. The tree is willing to lose the initial battles in order to win the war.[7]

This is a wonderful illustration of the formational power of the space between. Richard Foster has famously said that 'the desperate need today is not for a greater number of intelligent people, or gifted people, but for deep people'.[8] There can be no doubt of this: God produces deep people in the space between.

Second, we can trust that God will lead us from darkness into light. As Corrie ten Boon has said, 'When a train goes through a tunnel and it gets dark, you don't throw away the ticket and jump off. You sit still and trust the engineer.' Because of the hope of the resurrection, we know that our liminal seasons of life *will* become luminal, whether we see it on this side of eternity or the next. In Latin, *limen* means 'threshold', while *lumen* means 'an opening' or 'light'. Our time in the space between – on the threshold, in the darkness – will one day give way to an opening where we see shafts of light breaking through again. Our waiting will give way to fulfilment, our exile to homecoming, our wilderness to new life, our storm to peace and our pit to restoration. We will find new orientation, renewed identity, fresh structure for living and energy to engage again in a world reenchanted.

A friend from our church in Preston – who enjoys canal boating – shared a picture that she believed God gave her during one of our 24/7 times of prayer during the first coronavirus lockdown:

> *It was a picture of a tunnel on a canal that was long and unpleasant to journey through.*
>
> *When you enter, the massive metal doors clang shut behind you and the only light is from the boat's internal lights. Then the massive fume extractor fans start up and you are surrounded by this huge noise in almost pitch black. It is cold and dank.*
>
> *After a short while, far, far ahead you spot a tiny twinkle – no more than a pin prick. What a sight that is! And very slowly you are making your way towards this light. Your 15-ton canal boat is going to pass through this pin prick of light.*
>
> *Along the way there are ventilation shafts reaching up to ground level which give you quick glimpse of the world above as you sail past.*

I think God gave me this picture in detail to describe the corona-virus pandemic as the tunnel, the shafts as signs on the way that we are coming through and the light in sight is our Lord himself, drawing us to Him in this dark time.

Praise you, Lord Jesus!

We know from Psalm 139 that what seems like darkness to us looks entirely different from God's perspective:

Where can I go from your Spirit?
Where can I flee from your presence?
If I go up to the heavens, you are there;
if I make my bed in the depths, you are there.
If I rise on the wings of the dawn,
if I settle on the far side of the sea,
even there your hand will guide me,
your right hand will hold me fast.
If I say, 'Surely the darkness will hide me
and the light become night around me,'
even the darkness will not be dark to you;
the night will shine like the day,
for darkness is as light to you.
PSALM 139:7–12

God is revealed to be the inescapable God. There is not only light at the end of the tunnel, but light in the tunnel as well – even if it is not always light that we have the ability to see. Yet he will lead us through.

Finally, and ultimately, we can trust that God will never let us go. Henri Nouwen provides us with the most wonderful illustration of what it means to trust. He describes an encounter with 'The Flying Rodleighs', trapeze artists in a German circus. Nouwen went to see them in action with his father and then had the privilege of getting to know them on the road, as he became friends with them. He was intrigued to learn the art of the trapeze – of flying and catching.

One day, I was sitting with Rodleigh, the leader of the troupe, in his caravan, talking about flying. He said, 'As a flyer, I must have complete trust in my catcher. The public might think that I am the great star of the trapeze, but the real star is Joe, my catcher. He has to be there for me with split-second precision and grab me out of the air as I come to him in the long jump.'

'How does it work?' I asked.

'The secret,' Rodleigh said, 'is that the flyer does nothing and the catcher does everything. When I fly to Joe, I have simply to stretch out my arms and hands and wait for him to catch me and pull me safely over the apron behind the catchbar.'

'You do nothing!' I said, surprised.

'Nothing,' Rodleigh repeated. 'The worst thing the flyer can do is to try to catch the catcher. I am not supposed to catch Joe. It's Joe's task to catch me. If I grabbed Joe's wrists, I might break them, or he might break mine, and that would be the end for both of us. A flyer must fly, and a catcher must catch, and the flyer must trust, with outstretched arms, that his catcher will be there for him.'[9]

Nouwen reflects that, when Rodleigh said this with so much conviction, the words of Jesus flashed through his mind: '"Father, into your hands I commend my Spirit" (Luke 23:46). Dying is trusting in the catcher. To care for the dying [and, we should say, the living too] is to say, "Don't be afraid. Remember that you are the beloved child of God. He will be there when you make your long jump. Don't try to grab him; he will grab you. Just stretch out your arms and hands and trust, trust, trust."'

John Wesley's covenant prayer

I am no longer my own but yours.
Put me to what you will,
rank me with whom you will;
put me to doing,

put me to suffering;
let me be employed for you,
or laid aside for you,
exalted for you,
or brought low for you;
let me be full,
let me be empty,
let me have all things,
let me have nothing:
I freely and wholeheartedly yield all things
to your pleasure and disposal.
And now, glorious and blessed God,
Father, Son and Holy Spirit,
you are mine and I am yours. So be it.
And the covenant now made on earth, let it be ratified in heaven.
John Wesley

Questions for reflection

1   Which of the five metaphors in the book has most resonated for you? Why do you think this might be?
2   Which of the nine practices in this chapter connects with you at the moment? Journal anything that comes from these sections.
3   What of your past, present or future do you now see differently because of reading this book?

Words from Karen Fowler, illustrator

I have always learnt visually. Exams were perfect for me, as I could recall the pages of notes or textbooks in my mind's eye with coloured blobs or pictures on pages which unlocked the answers; whether I understood what I recalled was another matter. This is also the way the Holy Spirit enlightens me, catches my attention and takes me on a visual journey, but then gives me deeper revelation of what that means. As I was reading through *The Space Between*, my mind was alive with imagery, and as my rough sketches came together, I realised that there was a theme emerging: the circle.

Universally recognised. A symbol of both completeness and emptiness; of movement and solidity; of independence and covenant; of inclusivity and exclusivity. A circle is only a circle due to the space in the centre and the boundary at the edge. Space contained and space surrounding. It is this fundamental shape that is the starting point for each sketch; the fire kindled by the space between and the doorway into the book. A glimpse of hope to come or the safety of security.

Chapter 2 sees the three nails of the cross; the marks made on the hands and feet of Jesus that provide the ultimate disruptive moment. Three in one. The point that provides the five lenses of grace through which we can view the seasons of our own lives. In 'The time of waiting', we contemplate the stars, just as Abram did. When the territory is unknown as we camp in 'The place of exile'; stepping out or settling in. Exposure, vulnerability, and dependence that is cultivated in 'The wilderness'. Carried along by 'The storm' and the overwhelming, relentless intensity. Culminating in 'The pit'; the deep place.

The contrast of light to darkness is the way out of the book; the light at the end of the tunnel and the reminder of the constant faithfulness of the sun… setting or rising, you know that this moment will pass and there is more to come. Full circle.

Notes

1 Introduction

1 Judy Brown, *A Leader's Guide to Reflective Practice* (Trafford, 2006), p. 4. Used by permission.

2 Cited by Stephen R. Covey in Pat Croce, *Lead or Get Off the Pot! The seven secrets of a self-made leader* (Simon & Schuster, 2004), p. xiv.

3 Caroline Welby, foreword to Judy Hirst, *A Kind of Sleepwalking: And waking up to life* (DLT, 2014).

4 'The Way' is woven as a thread through New Testament scripture in other, more subtle, instances as well. The gospel writer Mark alludes to it when he speaks of one who will come to prepare the 'way of the Lord', drawing on a powerful theme in Isaiah (40:3). As Jesus journeys with his disciples from Galilee in the north of Israel to Jerusalem in the south (Mark 8:22—10:52), Mark makes particular use of 'the way'. On several occasions, Mark refers to 'the way' as he narrates how Jesus predicts his suffering, death and resurrection. Each time, the disciples demonstrate their 'blindness' in misunderstanding him, and Jesus teaches them what it means to follow him (Mark 8:27; 9:33–34; 10:17, 32, 46, 52). Compare Acts 9:2; 19:9, 23; 22:4; 24:14, 22. In contrast, the title 'Christians' that we are so familiar with today is only used three times in the whole of the New Testament – Acts 11:26; 26:28; 1 Peter 4:16.

5 This acronym was first used in 1987, drawing on the leadership theories of Warren Bennis and Burt Nanus.

6 William Bridges, *Transitions: Making sense of life's changes* (Lifelong Books, 2020), pp. 112–27.

7 Arnold van Gennep, *The Rites of Passage* (PUB, 1977), p. 21.

8 Bjørn Thomassen, 'The uses and meaning of liminality', *International Political Anthropology* 2.1 (2009), p. 51.

9 Bridges, *Transitions*, p. 145.

10 Richard Rohr, 'Days without answers in a narrow space', *National Catholic Reporter*, February 2002.

11 See **nextreformation.com/wp-admin/resources/liminal.pdf**

12 M. Scott Peck, *The Road Less Travelled* (Arrow, 1990), p. 11.

13 Walter Brueggemann, quoted at the Emergent Convention, Atlanta, Georgia, 16 September 2004.

14 N.T. Wright, *The New Testament and the People of God* (SPCK, 1992), p. 123.

15 Metaphors naturally overlap and interchange. For example, Israel's experience of exile is described in scripture as being like a wilderness (e.g. Isaiah 35:1–10).

16 This prayer is often attributed to Sir Francis Drake but is likely written by a gentleman named M.K.W. Heicher, according to **suburbanbanshee.wordpress.com/2011/11/18/sir-francis-drake-didnt-say-it**.

2 Two disruptive moments in the life of Jacob

1 Walter Wink, 'Prayer and the powers', *Sojourners Magazine* (October 1990), p. 13.

2 A.W. Tozer, *The Knowledge of the Holy* (HarperCollins, 1978), p. 1.

3 This is something of the meaning of the name 'YHWH' by which God reveals himself to Israel. Difficult to translate, it equates to something like 'I am who I am' or 'I will be whatever I will be'. It speaks of self-existence and otherness.

3 The time of wating: when life is put on hold

1 **youtube.com/watch?v=eghvMDmCpHE**

2 Walter Brueggemann, *The Message of the Psalms: A theological commentary* (Augsburg, 1984).

3 **tragedyandcongregations.org.uk**

4 Walter Brueggemann, *Spirituality of the Psalms* (Fortress Press, 2001), pp. 9–10.

5 Walter Brueggemann, 'The costly loss of lament', in Walter Brueggemann and Patrick Miller (eds), *The Psalms and the Life of Faith* (Fortress Press, 1995), pp. 98–111.

6 Walter Brueggemann, *From Whom No Secrets Are Hid: Introducing the Psalms* (Westminster John Knox Press, 2014), p. 92.

7 Walter Brueggemann, 'The Friday voice of faith', *CTJ* 36 (2001), p. 15.

8 Brueggemann, 'The costly loss of lament', p. 105.

9 Scott A. Ellington, *Risking Truth: Reshaping the world through prayers of lament* (Pickwick Publications, 2008), p. 7.

10 See the next chapter for an exploration of the importance of pilgrimage in the space between.

11 There are seven such 'penitential psalms' in the psalter. The other six are Psalms 6, 32, 38, 51, 102 and 143.

12 This is akin to what we are calling in this book 'the pit', which shows the overlap of these different metaphors of liminality. See chapter 7 on the pit.

13 The impatience of waiting in Psalm 130 is beautifully contrasted with the stillness of waiting in Psalm 131 and its image of a baby nursing on its mother who is content and settled. The baby knows it has nothing to worry about; so it can be for those who wait on the Lord.

14 Brueggemann, *From Whom No Secrets Are Hid*, p. 108.

15 Henri Nouwen, 'A spirituality of waiting', in John S. Mogabgab (ed.), *The Weavings Reader: Living with God in the world* (Upper Room Books, 1993), pp. 65–74.

16 **internetmonk.com/archive/adventii-sinais-last-thunder**

17 Eugene H. Peterson, *Earth and Altar: The community of prayer in a self-bound society* (IVP, 1985), pp. 35.

18 Michael Green, *Thirty Years That Changed the World: A fresh look at the book of Acts* (IVP, 2002), p. 44.

19 Sherry Turkle's TED talk 'Connected, but alone?' is powerful in drawing attention to the detrimental effects of social media: **ted. com/talks/sherry_turkle_connected_but_alone**.

20 The speech can be found at **sahistory.org.za/archive/speech-nelson-mandela-zionist-christian-church-easter-conference-moria-3-april-1994**

21 **crosswalk.com/devotionals/your-daily-prayer/a-prayer-for-when-you-re-stuck-in-the-waiting-place-your-daily-prayer-june-5-2017. html** – used with permission.

4 The place of exile: when life feels alien

1 Sang-Jin Han (ed.), *Divided Nations and Transitional Justice: What Germany, Japan and South Korea can teach the world* (Routledge, 2015), p. 60.

2 Margaret Silf, *Landmarks: An Ignatian journey* (DLT, 1998), p. 29.

3 Eugene H. Peterson, *Run with the Horses: The quest for life at its best* (IVP, 2010), p. 148.

4 Sotirios Christou, *The Psalms: Intimacy, doxology and theology* (Phoenix Books, 2012), p. 106.

5 Walter Brueggemann, *The Message of the Psalms: A theological commentary* (Augsburg, 1984), p. 75.

6 Jim Collins, *Good to Great: Why some companies make the leap... and others don't* (HarperCollins, 2001), pp. 83–87.

7 Marie-Jose Baudinet, 'The face of Christ, the form of the church', in

Michel Feher, Ramona Naddaff and Nadia Tazi (eds), *Fragments for a History of the Human Body, Part One* (Zone, 1989), p. 151.

8 To look into this book more, I recommend Ian Paul, *Revelation: An introduction and commentary*, Tyndale New Testament Commentaries (IVP, 2018) as well as Michael Wilcock, *The Message of Revelation*, The Bible Speaks Today (IVP, 1991). Eugene Peterson's *Reversed Thunder: The Revelation of John and the praying imagination* (Harper and Row, 1988) is also a great read.

9 For more information, see Wes Howard-Brook and Anthony Gwyther, *Unveiling Empire: Reading Revelation then and now* (Orbis Books, 1999).

10 For an introduction to Revelation's powerful use of numbers, see Paul, *Revelation*, pp. 34–39.

11 Tom Wright, *Surprised by Hope* (SPCK, 2008), p. 52.

12 See St John Chrysostom, Homily 24, On the Baptism of Christ.

13 Robert Webber, *Ancient-Future Time: Forming spirituality through the Christian year* (Baker Publishing Group, 2009), pp. 90–93.

14 I have also appreciated Tom Wright's more trinitarian focus in his Prayer of the Trinity. See **ntwrightpage.com/2016/04/05/the-prayer-of-the-trinity**.

15 Webber, *Ancient-Future Time*, p. 92.

16 William Bridges, *Transitions: Making sense of life's changes* (Lifelong Books, 2020), p. 136

17 Martin Robinson, *Sacred Places, Pilgrim Paths: An anthology of pilgrimage* (Fount, 1998), p. 127.

18 Perhaps another way to explore this would be to choose to serve in an 'alien' or unfamiliar place as a means of encountering others, God and ourselves. I found this when I did a placement in a prison – an environment that was entirely unfamiliar to me!

19 Frédéric Gros, *A Philosophy of Walking*, translated by John Howe (Verso, 2014), p. 107.

20 Mark Sayers, *Disappearing Church: From cultural relevance to gospel resilience* (Moody, 2016), p. 74.

21 Margaret J. Wheatley, *Leadership and the New Science: Discovering order in a chaotic world* (Berrett-Koehler Publishers, 2006).

22 See Arnold J. Toynbee, *A Study of History* (Oxford University Press, 1946).

23 Sayers, *Disappearing Church*, p. 156.

24 J. Robert Clinton, *The Making of a Leader: Recognising the lessons and stages of leadership development* (NavPress, 1988), p. 44.

25 **ststephenssociety.com**

26 Sam Hailes, 'Jackie Pullinger: "We're going to feel stupid for eternity if we waste this life"', *Premier Christianity*, January 2019, **premierchristianity.com/Past-Issues/2019/January-2019/Jackie-Pullinger-We-re-going-to-feel-stupid-for-eternity-if-we-waste-this-life**.

5 The wilderness: when life is stripped back

1 Mark Ireland and Mike Booker, *Making New Disciples: Exploring the paradoxes of evangelism* (SPCK, 2015), p. 68.

2 Antoine de Saint-Exupéry, *The Little Prince*, translated by Irene Testot-Ferry (Wordsworth Classics, 1995), p. 89.

3 David Runcorn, *The Road to Growth Less Travelled* (Grove Books S104, 2008), p. 10.

4 Ireland and Booker, *Making New Disciples*, p. 68.

5 John Mark Comer, *The Ruthless Elimination of Hurry: How to stay emotionally healthy and spiritually alive in the chaos of the modern world* (Hodder and Stoughton, 2019), p. 125.

6 Mike Pilavachi, *Wasteland? Encountering God in the desert* (David C. Cook, 2020), p. 26.

7 **internetmonk.com/archive/54579**

8 Thomas Merton, *Seasons of Celebration* (Farrar, Straus and Giroux, 2010), p. 13.

9 Christine Sine, 'Lent – not denial but transformation', posted on 4 March 2014, **godspacelight.com/2014/03/04/lent-not-denial-but-transformation**

10 C.S. Lewis, *The Complete Chronicles of Narnia* (HarperCollins, 2000), p. 321.

11 Lewis, *The Complete Chronicles of Narnia*, p. 321.

12 Luther, *Large Catechism*, IV:84–86; BC466–467.

13 Robert Webber, *Ancient-Future Time: Forming spirituality through the Christian year* (Baker Publishing Group, 2009), p. 113.

14 Ian Paul, 'How often did Jesus and his followers fast?', posted on 1 September 2016, **psephizo.com/biblical-studies/how-often-did-jesus-and-his-followers-fast**.

15 Paul, 'How often did Jesus and his followers fast?'

16 Richard J. Foster, *Celebration of Discipline* (Hodder and Stoughton, 2012), p. 71.

17 Webber, *Ancient-Future Time*, p. 114.

18 Such a dynamic might seem counter-intuitive, yet during the Covid-19 lockdown a movement of 'silent Zooms' helped many with

their concentration.

19   Benedicta Ward (trans.), *The Sayings of the Desert Fathers* (Cistercian Publications, 1975), p. 3.

20   'A Song of the Wilderness' in *Common Worship: Daily Prayer* © The Archbishops' Council 2005 and published by Church House Publishing. Used with permission.

6   The storm: when life is shaken

1   Haruki Murakami, *Kafka on the Shore* (Vintage, 2005), p. 4.

2   **shop.charliemackesy.com/item/the-best-thing-about-storms/print**

3   Dave Smith, *God's Plan For Your Wellbeing: 50-day guide* (Waverley Abbey Resources, 2020), p. 34.

4   Richard J. Foster, *Celebration of Discipline* (Hodder and Stoughton, 2012), p. 33.

5   Walter Brueggemann, *The Message of the Psalms: A theological commentary* (Augsburg, 1984). p. 123.

6   John Stott, *The Cross of Christ* (IVP, 1986), pp. 63–64.

7   Stott, *The Cross of Christ*, p. 64.

8   See Robert Webber, *Ancient-Future Time: Forming spirituality through the Christian year* (Baker Publishing Group, 2009), pp. 131–34 for more information on these.

9   The 14 stations are: (1) Jesus is condemned to death; (2) Jesus accepts the cross; (3) Jesus falls the first time; (4) Jesus meets his mother; (5) Simon of Cyrene carries the cross; (6) Veronica wipes the face of Jesus; (7) Jesus falls the second time; (8) Jesus meets the women of Jerusalem; (9) Jesus falls the third time; (10) Jesus is stripped of his garments; (11) Crucifixion: Jesus is nailed to the cross; (12) Jesus dies on the cross; (13) Jesus' body is removed from the cross; and (14) Jesus is laid in the tomb and covered in incense. Some churches add a resurrection scene.

10   The seven last sayings of Jesus are: (1) Luke 23:34: 'Father, forgive them, for they do not know what they are doing'; (2) Luke 23:43: 'Truly I tell you, today you will be with me in paradise'; (3) John 19:26–27: 'Woman, here is your son… Here is your mother'; (4) Matthew 27:46 and Mark 15:34: 'My God, my God, why have you forsaken me?'; (5) John 19:28: 'I am thirsty'; (6) John 19:30: 'It is finished'; (7) Luke 23:46: Father, into your hands I commit my spirit.'

11   Carla Grosch-Miller, 'Meditation on lament', posted on 10 May 2020, **tragedyandcongregations.org.uk/2020/05/10/meditation-on-lament-by-carla-grosch-miller**.

12 Biblical psalms of individual lament: 3—5, 7, 9—10, 13—14, 17, 22, 25—28, 31, 36, 39, 40:12–17, 41, 42—43, 52—57, 59, 61, 64, 70—71, 77, 86, 89, 120, 139, 141—142.

13 Biblical psalms of communal lament: 12, 44, 58, 60, 74, 79—80, 83, 85, 89—90, 94, 123, 126, 129.

14 Walter Brueggemann, *Spirituality of the Psalms* (Fortress Press, 2001), p. 27.

15 Dietrich Bonhoeffer, *Letters and Papers from Prison* (SCM Press, 1994), p. 359.

16 John Swinton, *Raging with Compassion: Pastoral responses to the problem of evil* (Eerdmans, 2007), p. 128.

17 **banneroftruth.org/uk/resources/articles/2001/john-newtons-conversion**

18 James Martin, 'A prayer in the storm', **americamagazine.org/faith/2012/10/28/hurricane-prayer**, reprinted from America October 28, 2012 with permission of America Press, Inc., 2012. All rights reserved.

7 The pit: when life sinks to the bottom

1 Quoted in Corrie ten Boom, *The Hiding Place* (Hodder & Stoughton, 2004).

2 Aleksandr Solzhenitsyn, *The Gulag Archipelago: 1918–1956*, Vol. 2 (Westview Press, 1997), pp. 615–17.

3 Walter Brueggemann, *Spirituality of the Psalms* (Fortress Press, 2001), p. 78.

4 Frederick Buechner, 'Prophet', posted on 21 April 2016, **frederickbuechner.com/quote-of-the-day/2016/4/21/prophet**.

5 Tom Wright, *Matthew for Everyone* (SPCK, 2002), p. 124.

6 See Henri Nouwen 'A spirituality of waiting', pp. 70–74.

7 John A.T. Robinson, *The Human Face of God* (Westminster Press, 1973), p. 131.

8 A.J. Swoboda, *A Glorious Dark: Finding hope in the tension between belief and experience* (Baker Books, 2015), p. 227.

9 Jonathan Storment, 'Awkward Holy Saturday', posted on 1 April 2015, **patheos.com/blogs/jesuscreed/2015/04/01/awkward-holy-saturday-jonathan-storment**

10 Andy Wade, 'Even resurrection pauses For sabbath rest', posted on 30 March 2013, **godspace.wordpress.com/2013/03/30/even-resurrection-pauses-for-sabbath-rest**

11 Kimberlee Conway Ireton, *The Circle of the Seasons: Meeting God in*

the church year (InterVarsity Press, 2008), p. 82.

12 Tom Wright, *Paul for Everyone: Romans, part 1 – chapters 1–8* (SPCK, 2006), p. 155.

13 The word 'apophatic' comes from the Greek word *apo* meaning 'other than' and the Greek word *phanai* meaning 'speak'.

14 For a modern take on sacred spaces, see George Lings, *Seven Sacred Spaces: Portals to deeper community life in Christ* (BRF, 2020).

15 Hugh Sykes, 'Ex-hostage Waite free from bitterness', *BBC News*, 19 February 2004, **news.bbc.co.uk/1/hi/world/middle_east/3503239. stm**.

16 Terry Waite, 'A spiritual journey', *The Friend*, 27 September 2018, **thefriend.org/article/a-spiritual-journey**.

17 Richard J. Foster and James Bryan Smith (ed.), *Devotional Classics: Selected readings for individuals and groups* (HarperCollins, 2005), p. 39.

18 Ann Weems, *Psalms of Lament* (Westminster John Knox Press, 1995), pp. 1–2. Used with permission.

8 Conclusion

1 Tom Wright, *Simply Good News: Why the gospel is news and what makes it good* (SPCK, 2015), p. 154.

2 Richard Rohr, 'Days without answers in a narrow space', *National Catholic Reporter*, February 2002.

3 See also William Bridges, *Transitions: Making sense of life's changes* (Lifelong Books, 2020), pp. 146–56, and Terry B. Walling, 'Out of the box [postures of transformation]', posted on 9 April 2020, **terrywalling.com/2020/04/09/out-of-the-box-postures-of-transformation**.

4 Barbara Fredrickson, *Positivity: Groundbreaking research to release your inner optimist and thrive* (One World, 2017), p. 41.

5 For more on the centrality of Easter, see Mark Bradford, *Encountering the Risen Christ: From Easter to Pentecost – the message of the resurrection and how it can change us* (BRF, 2016).

6 Mark Sayers, *Disappearing Church: From cultural relevance to gospel resilience* (Moody, 2016), p. 71.

7 Sayers, *Disappearing Church*, pp. 72–73.

8 Richard J. Foster, *Celebration of Discipline* (Hodder and Stoughton, 2012), p. 1.

9 Henri Nouwen, *Our Greatest Gift: A meditation on dying and caring* (John Murray Press, 2016), p. 66.